Privileged Information

Privileged Information

BY
TOM ALIBRANDI

WITH
FRANK H. ARMANI

DODD, MEAD & COMPANY
New York

Library of Congress Cataloging in Publication Data

Alibrandi, Tom.
  Privileged information.

    1. Garrow, Robert, 1936?–1978.   2. Trials (Murder)—
New York (State)—Syracuse.   3. Confidential communica-
tions—Lawyers—United States.   4. Armani, Frank H.
I. Armani, Frank H.   II. Title.
KF224.G378A44   1984   345.73′02523   84-1462
ISBN 0-396-08363-3   347.3052523

Acknowledgments

My mother and father, for their loving support while I wrote this book, and always.

Mary Ellen Jecman, Jay Wiley, Ed Kron, Robert Lundquist, Kevin McCarthy, Bob Earll, Russ Heblack, Mike O'Toole, and Mike and Sally Fitzpatrick, for their trust, faith and care.

Chuck Woll, Joe Garcia, Tom McGranahan and my other friends at Janus.

Frank Armani for asking me to write this story with him.

Clyde Taylor for believing in me.

T.A.

Tom Alibrandi, for his patience with me during the writing of this book.

My high school physics teacher and coach, Al Talmadge, for instilling a sense of discipline within me.

Monsignor Carl Denti, for teaching me my religious philosophy.

Dean Ralph Kharis, Honorable Frank Del Vecchio, Honorable Leo Hayes, Honorable George Marthen, Colonel Joseph Fournier, Colonel William Masterpoole, Eugene Pryor, Esq., and Elliot Taikeff, Esq.

My family, for their love, example and counsel; I have tried to live up to their expectations of me.

F.H.A.

Prologue

In PAST YEARS, many have asked why I did not immediately write a book about confidentiality and the Garrow case. Although I felt a great need to tell my story and, possibly as a result, purge my soul of its anguish, I was reluctant to do so. The pain of reliving that part of my past seemed too immense. Now, after ten years, I have written this book with Tom Alibrandi. I hope it will serve as a model for young attorneys called upon to defend *unpopular people* and *unpopular causes*. I hope it proves an inspiration to lawyers and judges with faith, courage, and an understanding of our Constitution, for our Constitution will be tested again and again by unpopular people and unpopular causes.

During the summer of 1973, my good friend Francis Belge and I were court appointed to defend Robert Garrow, the accused in a murder trial. The defense was "insanity." During the course of the trial, it became known that Garrow had told us of the location of two previously undiscovered bodies and that we did not pass on this information to the authorities or the parents of the victims when approached by them. It was further learned that we attempted to use this information in plea bargaining on behalf of our client, Robert Garrow.

The public was shocked by our seemingly callous conduct and our apparent lack of simple decency, and public rage was further inflamed by the prosecutors, who sought to indict us for

1

failing to reveal knowledge of the crimes and for failing to see
that the bodies were properly buried. To our chagrin and dis-
may, respected lawyers and law professors gave ambivalent and
confused responses when questioned on the issue by the press.
These lawyers included noted criminal authorities as well as
presidents of bar associations.

The fact that respected lawyers would comment to the press
while the trial was in process, and especially while disbarment
proceedings were pending against us, made me feel less than
secure with the position we had taken. It became apparent to
us that few members of the legal profession had given much serious thought to or understood the fundamental question that
was really at issue. Oh yes, there were a few like Monroe Fried-
man, dean of Hofstra Law School, and occasional attorneys
like Elliot Taikoff who sent messages of encouragement.

At that time, all we had to go on in defending ourselves was
our own moral upbringing and the oath of office we had taken
when sworn in as attorneys: ". . . that I will uphold the Constitution of the United States and the Constitution of the State of
New York and that I will maintain the confidence and preserve
inviolate the secrets of my client." To Belge and me, this oath
was and is a serious matter, a sacred trust. At the time we took
our oath of office, neither of us had the slightest idea of the
awesome consequences it would someday carry.

When I attended Syracuse University College of Law, and
when Francis Belge attended Albany Law School, there were
no courses in professional responsibility at most law schools.
Today, as a result of the case described in this book, professional responsibility is taught in every law school of any significance and is covered in the bar examination.

Our attempt to live up to the oath caused us, individually
and jointly with our families, great anguish and pain. Acts of
vandalism were committed against our properties, we received
death threats, and our children were humiliated at school. We
were vilified by certain news media. One editorial, which
brought me to tears, said we made the Watergate conspirators
look like Sunday school picnickers.

As a father of daughters, it was easy to empathize with the
victims' parents. I did feel a sense of moral compulsion to assist
them and to afford the victims the dignity of a decent burial.
But what was not understood by many who focused on these

details in the heat of the moment was that my obligation to my client was a vital issue with broader implications. I was under an obligation to the oath of office I had taken as an attorney at law to uphold the Constitution of the United States; I had committed myself to a system of administering justice that I believe is in itself absolutely essential to maintaining human dignity and the fundamentals of a free society. An essential element of this system is the *right to counsel with an attorney.* The right to counsel would be meaningless if the accused was not able always to communicate freely and fully with his lawyer. In order to protect that right of communication, there has been imposed upon us the sacred trust of confidentiality. That right of confidentiality—of privileged information—must exist even for unpopular people and causes, or it exists for no one.

In the beginning, Belge and I had no idea where this gruesome trail and trial would lead us. Looking back now, I know that, obliged by the trust of confidentiality, I would take the same path today.

I hope that you, the reader, will come to the same conclusion.

Frank H. Armani

"Confidentiality between lawyer and client is a privilege established in legal history, written in the code of professional responsibility for the American Bar Association and adopted as law in 48 of the 50 states. The oath of admission to the bar—proposed by the ABA and adopted in many states—requires lawyers to 'solemnly swear' that 'I will maintain the confidence and preserve inviolate the secrets of my client.' Violation of the oath can lead to disbarment."*

* "Ethical Dilemma: Should Lawyers Turn in Clients?" *Los Angeles Times*, July 2, 1974—feature article investigating Attorney Frank H. Armani's ethics in the Garrow case.

1

Sunday · July 29, 1973

THE ADIRONDACK MOUNTAINS in northern New York State between Wells and Speculator appeared more shadow than substance against the lavender early dawn sky. It was still mostly dark in the small clearing adjacent to old Route 8 where two lone tents were pitched. A 1970 blue Maverick and a 1968 orange Camaro were parked nearby on the shoulder of the road.

A high-pitched zipping sound broke the silence; then the flap of one of the tents was pushed open from the inside. Two young men crawled groggily out of the tent and stood barefoot in the weeds. Each sported shoulder-length dark hair and a full mustache, and each wore only briefs-style underpants.

They took a moment to survey their campsite. It had been raining late the night before when, after finding all of the nearby private and state campgrounds full, they had pulled off the highway and pitched their tents. Nick Fiorello, age twenty, and Philip Domblewski, eighteen, felt good about where they had camped. The clearing was bordered by dense woods on three sides, and on the fourth by the macadam road. They would have plenty of privacy.

The two of them reached inside the tent for their clothes. Then they silently dressed, took down their tent, and gathered their fishing gear. When finished, they paused to take in the

5

pungent, piney smells and the rugged beauty. They listened to the soft rippling of a nearby stream and to the singing of a solitary bird. Beyond that, each heard only the beating of his own pulse. Both young men loved the Adirondacks; they were grateful to be away from their muggy hometown of Schenectady for the weekend. For Domblewski, this camping trip had a special significance—it was a gift to himself for graduating from high school the previous month.

Domblewski broke the meditative moment. He turned his heavy-lidded, brown eyes toward the other tent and called, "We're goin' fishing, Dave. You guys want to come along? Or you gonna sleep all day?"

"What time is it?" David Freeman mumbled from inside the tent.

"A little after six," Fiorello answered.

There was a groan from inside the tent.

Domblewski laughed. "We'll only be a couple of hours."

"See you when you get back. . . . And good luck," Freeman called. "We'll cook up what you catch for breakfast."

Inside the tent, Freeman turned back toward Carol Ann Malinowski, his slight of build, blond girl friend. He pulled the top of their double sleeping bag up over his shoulder and closed his eyes.

Domblewski and Fiorello piled into Fiorello's Maverick and headed into the nearby hamlet of Wells for bait and a hot cup of coffee. On the way into town, the two young men talked about how good it was to be spending the weekend in the woods with David Freeman. The trio had been buddies since childhood and had shared many fine times together. Even after Freeman had gotten serious over Carol Ann, he hadn't given up on his friends Nick and Phil. He wasn't like other guys from their group, to whom getting engaged or married meant a serious and inactive adulthood. Dave liked to include his two buddies in many of the plans he made with Carol Ann—like this camping trip. When Dave and Carol Ann had decided to spend this weekend in the mountains, they had asked his friends to come along.

Domblewski and Fiorello had been gone from the campsite for about three hours when a 1972 orange Volkswagen Fastback glided to a stop on the shoulder of old Route 8. The driver of the car, Robert Garrow, gazed out over the clearing. The sun

was well over the tree line, and the powder blue of David Freeman's tent seemed to glow against the forest's verdant lushness.

Garrow drove slowly along the road for another fifty feet. He
turned his VW into a second clearing in the forest on the opposite side of the highway from the campsite, then carefully
parked his car so that it was hidden from the road.

Garrow, thirty-six years old and powerfully built, pushed out
of his car and stretched to his full six feet. He slipped a pair of
binoculars around his neck and jammed a green felt hat on his
balding head. Then, after adjusting his holstered ten-inch Buck
knife so it rode comfortably on his right hip, he reached into
the backseat of his car and removed his hunting rifle.

He paused for a moment. He had a headache so bad it
nearly made him sick to his stomach. In an attempt to squeeze
off some of the mounting pain, he pressed his palms hard
against his temples. It didn't help much.

Garrow walked diagonally across the clearing with the quiet,
fluid grace of someone well-versed in moving undetected in the
wilds. He crossed the highway, cut through the trees, and made
for the campsite. Once there, he crouched silently in front of
the blue tent, and pushed his dark-rimmed glasses up against
his face—they had a habit of sliding down his nose when he
perspired heavily. Then he pulled the tent flap open with the
barrel of his rifle.

David Freeman and Carol Ann Malinowski, each wearing
only underpants, were lounging on top of their sleeping bag. It
took them a moment to realize that someone had violated their
privacy and was staring in at them.

"What the hell!" Freeman blurted upon seeing the man.

Carol Ann moved to cover herself with the sleeping bag;
Freeman instinctively slipped into his cutoff jeans. He figured
the man for a conservation agent. Even so, he didn't like the
idea that the guy was toting a rifle. Equally disturbing to Freeman were the man's piercing blue eyes; there was something
dangerous and forbidding about his stare. Deep inside Garrow's cloudy pupils was a faint glow, like that of a dying light
bulb.

"What do you want?" Freeman heard himself ask.

"My car ran out of gas down the road a bit," Garrow answered. "I want to siphon a couple of gallons out of that Camaro. Is it your car?"

"My girl friend's," Freeman answered.

While glaring at the young couple, Garrow had the sensation of rushing wind in his ears, and his head throbbed with pain. Deep in his mind, he saw another picture, different from the one he was seeing inside the tent. The picture was over fifteen years old but was still sharply focused. A nude woman in her late teens, slightly built and with small breasts, was in bed. On top of her, making love to her, was a long-haired young man. A teenaged, greasy-haired Garrow burst into the room; the woman began screaming. The long-haired young man of Garrow's memory jumped from the bed and squared off against the intruder.

Garrow blinked his eyes into focus, and his gaze locked on Carol Ann Malinowski for a long, frightening moment. "Are you two married?" he asked unexpectedly.

"No, we're not," Freeman answered weakly.

"What would your parents say if they knew you were carrying on like this?" Garrow asked, his tone soft, like that of a concerned adult steering two errant youngsters into a proper course of conduct.

"What business is it of yours, anyway?" Carol Ann demanded, her embarrassment giving way to anger.

"Get dressed and come out of there," Garrow ordered. Still in a crouched position, he held the tent flap open with the barrel of his gun in such a way that the weapon was pointed at the young couple.

Carol Ann was about to protest but stifled it when David handed her her clothes.

Garrow watched the young woman wiggle into cutoffs and a pullover tank top. When she'd finished, he stood and backed up so the couple could exit the tent.

"Come with me while I get the siphon hose out of my car," he instructed, sounding nervous but polite.

Freeman took this moment to register a closer look at the man who stood facing him. Garrow's red cotton shirt accentuated his wide shoulders, and his tan khaki pants clung to obviously muscular legs. This guy is a real bull, Freeman thought. Must be stronger than hell.

"Let's go," Garrow directed.

They turned toward the highway. Just then Nick Fiorello and Phil Domblewski arrived back at the campsite. Freeman felt instantly relieved. Something about this man deeply frightened him.

"Who's that?" Garrow asked, growing instantly agitated. He pushed his glasses up to the bridge of his nose and stared at the two young men walking toward him.

"Friends," Freeman answered. He suppressed the urge to signal Nick and Phil that trouble awaited them. David didn't want to excite the intruder further.

Garrow stepped aside as Nick and Phil joined them, so that all four young people were positioned in front of him.

"What's going on?" Domblewski asked. Eyeing the man's rifle and binoculars, he also figured Garrow for a conservation officer.

"He wants some gas . . ." Freeman started, but he trailed off when he glanced at Garrow. The man's face and neck were scarlet and looked as though they were about to burst.

"I'm going to siphon some gas from your cars," Garrow advised.

"Who says?" Domblewski objected.

Freeman flinched. Phil Domblewski wasn't afraid to stand up to anyone, but just now Freeman wished that Phil would avoid bumping egos with this guy. Let the man take as much gas as he wanted, if that would settle things. Then he could be on his way.

"I say you're gonna give me the gas," Garrow replied, almost cordially, while staring hard at Domblewski. Garrow acted like two separate, distinct people. One spoke cordially and quietly. The other seemed consumed by fury. Slowly but with clear menace, he raised his rifle toward the foursome.

Domblewski's eyes tightened, and he held his ground in front of the gun.

"Let's go. And don't try anything funny," Garrow said, gesturing his rifle in the direction of the highway. "I've killed before and I will again if I have to. The FBI and the state police are looking for me, and I have nothing to lose."

Shocked by this last statement, the young campers nervously eyed one another. When Freeman saw that Domblewski was about to protest further, he said in a shaky voice, "Do what he says, Phil."

Domblewski backed off. He fell into step with Freeman and Fiorello, who'd formed a partial circle around Carol Ann. Garrow walked a couple of paces behind and herded the group toward the road. They crossed the macadam highway and headed into the clearing where Garrow's car was parked.

"Look, man," Nick Fiorello said as they walked, "I understand your nervousness. I've been in trouble with the law before. Take what gas you want, and be on your way. We won't say anything to anybody. We'll just forget this thing happened."

Freeman glanced at Domblewski. Fiorello was lying about having been in trouble with the law. Their friend was trying to reason with the man.

Garrow offered no reply. Once they had reached his car, he removed a coil of rope from the front seat of the Volkswagen and ordered, "That way."

Realizing Garrow was forcing them into the woods, Domblewski demanded, "What the hell's goin' on? You don't want any gas."

"Just do what I tell you. And shut your mouth," Garrow snapped angrily.

"Easy, Phil," Fiorello cautioned.

For the second time, Domblewski acceded to a friend's warning and followed orders.

Garrow force-marched the group away from the highway and toward the woods. All the way across the clearing Freeman kept hoping that a car would come along, that someone would notice what was happening. But the road remained deserted.

After they had gone a few feet into the thick, punishing underbrush, Garrow ordered them to halt. He withdrew the Buck knife from the holster attached to his belt and cut a length of rope. He handed the rope to Fiorello and nodded toward Freeman.

"Tie him to this tree. And do it right."

A fearful Daniel Freeman stepped up to the tall maple tree. He put his arms around the trunk as if embracing it and kept his face flush against the bark while his friend wound the rope around his wrists and worked the ends of it into a knot. Freeman couldn't get over how calm Garrow acted. It was as if this man were reenacting some strange game he'd played many times before.

When Fiorello finished, Garrow herded the remaining trio farther into the woods. So dense was the foliage that they had only to walk a few feet before they were out of Freeman's range of vision. Garrow then had Domblewski tie Fiorello to a tree. Then he took Domblewski and Carol Ann to another spot deeper in the woods, out of Freeman's and Fiorello's sight.

"Okay," Garrow ordered the woman. "Tie him up here."

"What are you going to do with her, man?" Domblewski protested.

"Don't worry about it," Garrow answered.

"You better not touch her," Domblewski warned.

"Just get up against the tree," Garrow said, jabbing the gun muzzle into the small of the other's back. As an afterthought, he grabbed Domblewski's shoulder and spun him around so that he faced away from the tree. Florid-faced, Garrow stared menacingly at his captive.

"You better not mess with her, man," Domblewski said as Carol Ann tied his hands behind him.

Garrow simply smiled, then led a terrified Carol Ann into the underbrush. Once they were out of sight of the others, Garrow stopped in front of a diseased, leafless elm tree. He glanced down at Carol Ann's feet. Her moccasins were caked with mud from the walk across the clearing.

"I'm real sorry about your shoes," he said politely as he tied her so her back was to the tree.

"That's not too tight, is it?" he asked. "The rope isn't hurting your wrists?"

"No, it's okay," she answered shakily.

"Take it easy. Everything will be all right," Garrow assured. "I'm going to check the knots on the others, and I'll be right back."

From where he was tied, Phil Domblewski listened intently. He expected the worst; he was afraid he would hear Carol Ann cry out from being assaulted or raped. But there was only the murmur of low, muted voices. Then Garrow reappeared out of the trees, his rifle balanced in the crook of his left elbow.

As Garrow stepped to a spot in front of him, Domblewski, a look of frightened contempt on his face, said, "You've had your fun; now why don't you leave us alone."

Garrow reached out and slapped him hard across the face.

Domblewski's cheek instantly reddened from the blow. "Just wait until the cops get ahold of you for this, you bastard."

A small smile pulled at Garrow's lips. It was as if he had gotten the response he had hoped for. "Quite a mouth you have on you, hippy."

With the young man glaring back at him, Garrow removed the Buck knife from its holster. He held the razor-sharp knife lightly in his hand and waved it in front of Domblewski's face, as if proudly showing him how well balanced it was. While doing so, Garrow again heard that howling sound in his ears. His eyes widened and glazed over. His attention fixed on that memory from his adolescence. In it the small-breasted woman in bed was tearfully telling the teenaged Garrow that she no longer loved him, that she was in love with the long-haired man who'd been making love to her. Then the long-haired man began yelling at Garrow to get out of the house, or he would call the cops.

"Leave me alone, you bastard!" Domblewski yelled, bringing Garrow out of his thoughts. The teenager had scrunched his back against the tree to avoid the knife edge. Suddenly his leg lashed out, and he kicked Garrow flush on the knee.

"A real brave hippy," Garrow said, snarling.

Showing no evidence of being hurt by the kick, the older man stepped away. He placed his rifle down on the ground carefully, so as not to foul the gun's action. Then he squared off against Domblewski. With his Buck knife in his right hand, his lips worked into a small, hateful sneer, and with Domblewski kicking at him, Garrow lunged forward. He jammed his forearm against the young man's throat, pinning his head against the tree, and pointed his knife at Domblewski's chest.

Domblewski felt as though his neck was being crushed. His face only inches from his attacker's, he vainly tried twisting his head to get some air. His screams wound down to hoarse gasps. He kept frantically trying to kick his attacker in the groin.

Some twenty feet away from where Garrow struggled with Domblewski, Carol Ann strained against her bonds until her wrists burned. When Phil's yelling ceased, she went rigid. She heard a long vomiting sound, followed by a series of sickening choking gasps . . . then nothing.

"What are you doing to him?" Carol Ann called.

"It's okay. I'll be done in a minute," Garrow answered calmly.

The next thing the young woman knew, someone was crashing through the woods to her left. It was the wild running of a person or animal careening through the thick underbrush.

Carol Ann kept working against her bonds until her wrists and hands turned slick with sweat and she was able to free herself. Hearing nothing, she walked quietly in the direction from which Phil's yelling had come. When she got close enough to see through the underbrush and trees, she noted that Garrow was on one knee in front of Domblewski. Phil was seated on the ground, facing away from her, his back against the tree.

Confused and frightened, the young woman crouched low in the underbrush. She waited until Garrow retrieved his rifle and stalked into the woods. Then she waited some more . . . just to be sure.

Meanwhile, David Freeman had also worked loose from his bonds. He was making his way toward where he thought the others were when Garrow stepped out from behind a tree in front of him. Freeman froze.

"Your friend got away," Garrow said, his words coming in disjointed cadence. "You're going to help me find him."

"Who—" Freeman started to ask.

"Head that way," Garrow ordered, and he pointed with his rifle.

For the next fifteen minutes Garrow forced Freeman to walk in erratic circles through the forest. All during the search David kept wondering where the others were; he hoped that whoever had escaped had gone for help.

When they reached the clearing, Freeman saw immediately that Fiorello's Maverick was missing. Garrow also noticed and began studying the surrounding landscape. "All right, over there," he snapped. He motioned Freeman down into a ravine that ran along the line of trees.

They had reached the ravine floor and were just inside the edge of the forest when three cars slid to a stop on the shoulder of the highway. Freeman felt a surge of relief at hearing men pile out of the cars, slamming doors behind them. Then he heard Nick Fiorello's voice. His friend was directing the group to where the young campers had been tied up. In doing so, Fiorello led the dozen armed men along the ridge of the ravine to within a few yards of where Garrow was holding Freeman captive.

Freeman watched the line of men file by. Suddenly, in an unthinking, instinctive rush for survival, he lunged away from Garrow. Clutching at the tall grass, he scurried on all fours to the top of the ravine. "He's going to kill me! He's going to kill us all!" he screamed.

Fiorello's face was gray and gaunt with anxiety as he ran to his friend. "Where are the others? Where are Phil and Carol?"

"They must still be back in the woods," Freeman gasped.

The two friends started into the forest in search of their companions when the voice of one of the men who had driven back with Fiorello from Wells stopped them cold.

"There he is," the man barked, pointing.

Garrow, his rifle held tight against his chest, ran low to the ground across an open patch of sunlight. He veered right, away from the group of men, and disappeared into the forest.

"Phil and Carol are still in there," Freeman yelled, and he dashed into the woods.

Closely followed by Fiorello, Freeman led the men along the path of broken grass marking the route Garrow had taken the young campers along earlier, when he had forced them into the woods. They passed the trees to which the two escaped campers had been secured. The loose ropes were still looped around the base of their trunks. Then they came upon Phil Domblewski and Carol Ann Malinowski. Domblewski was sitting untied on the grassy floor, his back propped against the tree to which he had been secured. The rope was missing. Stuck in the ground next to him was Garrow's blood-smeared hunting knife.

Carol Ann was kneeling in front of her friend, staring at him and crying softly.

David Freeman rushed up to his girl friend. Then he looked at Domblewski. "Please, God, no!"

Domblewski's open mouth was drooling green mucousy matter. The front of his shirt, the area around his heart, was a wet clot of crimson.

Freeman knelt and placed a finger on his friend's neck. When he didn't get a pulse, he began crying, softly at first, then sobbing.

As the rest of the men gathered around the body, they heard a car start nearby. Robert Garrow had doubled back and was escaping in his Volkswagen.

2

Sunday Afternoon · July 29, 1973

Forty-six-year-old Frank Armani chugged up the marble stairs to the Syracuse Public Safety Building. Once inside the double glass doors, the stocky, five-foot-seven-inch tall attorney paused to mop his brow with his handkerchief. He dabbed carefully around the front of his gray-flecked black toupee. He had learned from embarrassing experience that to rub too hard or too carelessly at his forehead would flip the front of his hairpiece up in such a fashion as to make it plainly evident that he wore one. He then removed his smoky-colored plastic-rimmed glasses and wiped the perspiration from his face. His features were weathered, chiseled in the spirit of the ancient castle of Trento in his ancestral home in the Italian Dolomites. His face, depending on Armani's mood, was capable of expressing great gentleness and love, or fearsome turbulence.

He turned and headed down the long hallway to the jailer's cage, resenting that he had to work on Sunday. He would have preferred to be up at his place on Hill Island on the St. Lawrence River, where his wife and two daughters were whiling away the hot summer weekend. He wished his client had picked another night than Saturday to get drunk and beat up on his old lady. Armani smiled at that one. Attorneys were a lot like doctors, he thought—no set hours and unpredictable catastrophes. The difference was that doctors who were in the middle of enjoying their weekend referred their patients to a hospital emergency room. There were no emergency rooms for law clients in trouble, just jails.

He stepped up to the bulletproof glass. Eddie, the jailer, buzzed the electronically activated door and waved him in.

"Hello, Frank," the lanky cop greeted him. "Are the fish biting on the St. Lawrence?"

"If they are, Eddie, they are munching on someone else's bait," Armani kidded. He placed his thin leather briefcase on the counter.

"Who are you here to see?" Eddie asked.

"Joey Fitzgibbons."

"Ah, the middleweight champ of the women's division," Eddie said with a smile. He pushed the sign-in sheet across the counter.

"How's he doing?" Armani asked while scribbling his signature.

"Probably got enough cotton on his tongue by now to sew a shirt," the cop replied.

"That's my boy," Frank answered. He turned for the elevator that would bring him upstairs to the cellblock. He had taken about ten steps when Eddie's voice stopped him in his tracks.

"Oh, yeah, Armani. I almost forgot. You got a phone message. Investigator McCabe of the State Bureau of Criminal Investigation has been trying to get ahold of you."

"BCI?" Armani returned to the jailer's desk for the phone message slip. "What the hell they want with me on a Sunday?"

"Might have to do with your client Garrow," Eddie suggested.

"Garrow?"

"They're looking for him in the Adirondacks. Claim he killed a kid this morning near Speculator." Eddie's face was serious and his eyes sympathetic. No matter that he and Armani were on opposite sides of the legal fence, until any case was argued in court, the authorities and defense lawyers maintained a certain camaraderie about such matters.

"What?" Armani blurted.

"Kid's name is Philip Domblewski. He was camping with some friends who made the positive ID on Garrow a few hours ago. BCI also wants to talk with Garrow about some other killings and abductions that fit the pattern of the Domblewski murder. It's on all the wires."

"Incredible!" Armani exclaimed.

"Supposed to be one of the largest manhunts in the state's history." Eddie turned back to the bulletproof glass. Someone else was waiting to be let in.

Armani's fatigue gave way to an anxious feeling. He did an about-face and made his way slowly to the elevator.

Throughout his interview with the remorseful, hung over Joey Fitzgibbons and while he arranged for the posting of Fitzgibbons' bail, Armani couldn't get his mind off what he had just learned about Robert Garrow. The shocking news quashed any hopes Armani had of making the hour drive that afternoon to his rustic Hill Island summer home. There would be no dinner with his family, no returning well rested to his office sometime the following day. There was too much to do now.

Armani piloted the tan Mercedes sedan he had brought back from his recent European trip to his West Genesee Street law offices. Once seated at his desk, a manila file folder in front of him, he was now pleased that it was Sunday—there were no phone calls to disturb him, and none of the three lawyers or five secretaries who worked for him would be interrupting him for consultation about some matter. Though he had never before defended a murder suspect—assuming Robert Garrow would be charged with the murder for which he was being sought—Armani intuitively understood that things could get hectic over the next few days. He had better review Garrow's file so he could handle whatever was coming. He lit one of the fifty Salems he inhaled in a day, opened the folder, and started reading.

The first entry in the file was background information Armani had arranged to get after Garrow had been referred to him as a client. A November 6, 1961, *Albany Times-Union* article reported that Robert Garrow, then twenty-five years old, greasy-haired, and married with two children, had raped a teenage girl after knocking her high school football star boyfriend unconscious with the butt of a pellet gun. Garrow was arrested after a wild chase in which several shots were fired by the police. He was eventually convicted and served eight years in prison. Since his subsequent release from the penitentiary, Garrow had proven a good family man and neighbor and had compiled an excellent job record as master mechanic at Mill-brook Bakery. He was such a model parolee that he had once been studied by the New York State Crime Commission as an example of someone who broke the pattern of recidivism—most released prisoners routinely returned to prison for crimes similar to those of which they'd first been convicted.

Armani turned to the next entry in the file, the handwritten log of his own first contact with Robert Garrow. Garrow had come to his office in mid-August 1972, after a minor auto accident. Garrow had struck his head on the roof of his Volkswagen and suffered a minor injury for which he had refused medical treatment. He had been more concerned about the welfare of the passenger in his car at the time, a young neighbor boy who had been unharmed in the accident. So concerned was Garrow that he had wanted Armani to sue Garrow's insurance carrier for any possible future medical problems the boy might suffer as a result of the accident. Armani had declined on the basis that, since he represented Garrow, it would be a conflict of interest to sue his own client's insurance company. He had advised Garrow that the boy's family should retain their own attorney. As it happened, neither Garrow nor the boy's parents had taken any further action in the matter.

Armani studied the following page. It was dated November 10, 1972. Garrow had called him from the Syracuse Public Safety Building, where he was being held on charges of unlawful imprisonment and possession of a dangerous drug, crimes Garrow vehemently denied committing. The police report stated that Garrow had allegedly held two Syracuse University students, Karen Lutz and Leonard Garner, hostage at gunpoint and then tied them up. After Garrow had spent a couple of days in jail, it was ascertained that the bag of marijuana found under the front seat of his Volkswagen belonged to Lutz and Garner. When the two students refused to press formal charges against Garrow, he was released. The presiding judge, in dismissing the charges against Garrow, had stated that Garrow's exemplary record since being released from prison was in no way predictive of the aberrant behavior of which he'd been accused. By freeing Garrow and thus clearing his name, the judge said he was "righting a miscarriage of justice against Robert Garrow."

That one sent Frank Armani rocking back and forth in his chair. With the charges against Garrow dismissed, an action Armani had worked diligently to justify, the ex-convict could not be held in violation of his parole, so he had been spared from returning to prison. Thus if Garrow had killed that kid in the Adirondacks, he had been free to do it in part because, in representing his client's interests to the best of his ability, Frank Armani had been instrumental in allowing him to walk the streets.

Still looking away from the file folder on his desk, Armani was reminded of another incident, one that had happened only a few months before, on April 29, 1973. He had not thought it important enough at the time to document in Garrow's file.

Garrow had appeared in Armani's office to pay his legal bill. During that visit, Garrow had claimed to be able to foresee the future. He was concerned that his son, Robert, Jr., was going to get into serious trouble someday. (The boy was already a disciplinary problem in school.) Armani had discounted Garrow's claim as a common one. He himself had on occasion anticipated certain events that had eventually occurred. He had reassured Garrow that many kids who are disciplinary problems for a time in school straighten up after tasting the first consequences of their behavior.

Now that he thought about it, it was Garrow's manner that had troubled Armani more than anything else that day. His client had been highly agitated, speaking in a rambling, disjointed fashion. It was something Armani had shrugged off as a bout of nerves.

He let his gaze fall back to the file. There was one more sheet documenting his professional relationship with Robert Garrow.

On the first Saturday of June 1973, less than two months earlier, Armani had received a call from the police in Geddes, a Syracuse suburb, informing him that they had Robert Garrow in custody. Garrow had allegedly picked up two young girls aged ten and eleven and driven them to a secluded area, where he had them masturbate him and perform oral sex on him. Though Garrow again strongly denied his guilt, that time Armani had begun to wonder about his client. But after reading the girls' statements, the lawyer had been convinced that the girls had been coached—their statements had contained too much exact recall. They had described Garrow's features and manner of carrying himself with the kind of precise detail Armani would have had difficulty eliciting from most adults.

Based on his misgivings about the girls' statements, Armani had held to the hope that Garrow might be innocent, a victim of mistaken identity or even of police harrassment. It had happened before. The police had been known to be overzealous in building cases against known sex offenders in efforts to solve crimes involving children.

This time Armani didn't get the opportunity to defend his client in a court of law. After Garrow was arraigned on the child molestation charge, he was released on bail. Then he disappeared. He failed to show up for trial on July 23rd and again on the postponed date of July 26th that Armani had requested from the presiding judge. So a bench warrant had been issued on July 26th for Robert Garrow's arrest. That was just three days past.

Armani took a few minutes to smoke another cigarette and let the situation turn over in his head. Then he reached into his pocket for the phone message slip and dialed the number given on it.

"Investigator McCabe," came the voice over the phone.

"This is Frank Armani in Syracuse. You wanted to talk with me?"

"Armani! I've been looking all over the state for you . . . finally got ahold of your wife up north. You hear about Garrow?" McCabe had a strong New York accent—probably Brooklyn, Armani guessed—and spoke with the quiet authority of a veteran cop.

"Just," Armani responded, careful to let McCabe do the talking.

"We're moving an army of troopers and conservation officers up there to find him," the investigator revealed. "I was just about to leave the Glens Falls barracks for Speculator, and I need to know some things about your client."

"I'll try to help."

"We want to take him alive if possible, Armani. How dangerous is he?"

"Garrow showed me his prison record once," Armani said, remembering. "It said that he split a couple of guys' faces open like ripe melons, each time with a single punch. Nobody messed with him after that. Just by the looks of the guy, if I got into a fight with him, I'd want a weapon. What do you have on him?"

"Got him cold on the Domblewski murder," McCabe answered. Now he was obviously being cautious not to give away too much. "Plus we have an unsolved homicide near Weverton that fits the m.o. of the Domblewski murder. A kid named Porter was tied up and stabbed to death. Looks like the same rope was used in both crimes."

Armani recalled reading about the incident. On July 20th, Daniel Porter, twenty-one, of Boston had been found stabbed to death in the woods near Weverton, some fifty miles from the site of the Domblewski murder. Daniel Porter's camping companion, Susan Petz, a Boston College coed from Skokie, Illinois, had vanished without a trace.

"It's our guess that your client has got the Petz girl stashed somewhere," McCabe volunteered. "If she's in the woods, we're working against a maximum three-week survival time. We've got to find Garrow so he can lead us to her before the elements or starvation kill her."

"*If* he took her," Armani reminded.

"We've placed him in the area on the twentieth," McCabe added confidently. "Garrow will do as a suspect until something better comes up."

"Was there a girl among Domblewski's camping companions?" Armani asked hesitantly.

"A twenty-three-year-old woman named Carol Ann Malinowski," McCabe answered. "We figure Garrow was after her."

Armani let out a long breath and reached for another cigarette. "Let me know as soon as you get anything."

"The minute we do," McCabe agreed, and he hung up.

Armani leaned back in his chair. He tried to imagine Robert Garrow, the soft-spoken, round-faced bakery mechanic, as capable of murder. That was how Armani had been trained to think as a defense lawyer: Assume the worst and work backwards to the most plausible explanation for a client's suspected guilt. That way you got a line on the basis for the prosecution's case. Then you could build *your* case accordingly.

But all Frank Armani kept coming up with were questions about how he would handle something of this magnitude.

3

Early Evening · Sunday · July 29, 1973

IT WAS DUSK by the time Senior BCI Investigator Henry McCabe steered his unmarked gray Dodge into the parking lot behind the Hamilton County courthouse in Lake Pleasant. After locating an empty spot among the fleet of state police cars, he wearily climbed from his car and headed for the two-story jail located next door to the newer limestone and brick courthouse. The turn-of-the-century vintage stone jail, resembling a medieval fort with barred slits for windows, was being utilized for the search command post.

McCabe, in his late forties, six feet tall, red-faced and lean, waded through the knot of state troopers milling around the cluttered booking desk. He spotted Major Don Ambler leaning over the communications officer, who was busily monitoring calls from troopers in the woods.

Ambler glanced up and smiled as McCabe approached. None of the competition that existed between the regular state police and the elite BCI came into play with Ambler. The youthful-looking, sandy-haired, thin trooper was grateful that Henry McCabe had arrived to oversee the search. Ambler respected McCabe; the senior BCI investigator was a cop's cop. You got no fanfare or publicity hounding from McCabe, just thorough, efficient police work.

22

"What have you got, Don?" McCabe asked, reaching across the desk to shake Ambler's hand.

"Spaghetti," the uniformed officer answered. "I've got roadblocks sealing off the area, three hundred men crawling all over these mountains, and Garrow could be in the woods fifty feet from here and we'd never spot him, this terrain is so rugged. My biggest job so far has been to keep my men from getting lost out there."

McCabe nodded.

"This guy's tough as nails, and he knows these woods like his own backyard," Ambler added, running a hand through his thick unruly hair.

McCabe looked closely at the major; Ambler's bloodshot blue eyes showed the pressure he was under. All day long reports had filtered in about Garrow's credentials as a woodsman. The fugitive had been raised in the Adirondack village of Mineville and had spent most of his life hunting, fishing, and hiking in this sparsely populated, vast mountain range.

"Plus he doesn't want to get caught—a rough combination." McCabe provided the obvious critical detail. "Any sightings?"

"You kidding? About everyone in the area swears they saw Garrow lurking around their house or camp. People are evacuating these mountains in droves."

"Anything concrete?" McCabe prodded.

"A couple of definites. Earlier this afternoon, some woman passed a man in an orange Volkswagen fastback on Route Eight on the other side of Wells. When she reached our roadblock, she freaked out—guess the poor woman thought our boys were part of a Garrow gang. She pulled a U-turn and sped off. Lucky she wasn't shot. When we caught up to her, she explained about the orange VW and described Garrow. The bastard even slowed down to smile and wave when he passed her. He was long gone by the time we got the information from the woman."

"That it?" McCabe asked.

"One more sighting. About a half hour ago one of our guys spotted Garrow east of Wells. He gave chase for a couple of miles but lost him on the curves. Later another officer found Garrow's car stashed in the woods."

"You got his car?"

"Still in the woods, where he left it."

"Anybody touch it?" McCabe pressed.

"We been waiting for you to get here," Ambler answered, to McCabe's satisfaction.

"Let's get out there." McCabe turned to leave.

Once they were in the parking lot, out of earshot of the troopers in the command post, McCabe added, "I'd suggest you get your control operations out of the jail and into the woods, Don. We're looking for a guy who's on the move on foot. Chances are slim that he'd walk into the jailhouse. The only way to catch Garrow is to match him move for move in the woods, flush him out into the open where we have a chance at him. Let him remain in the woods, and Garrow is playing on his home court. He can hole up in the mountains and stay strong for a long time."

Fifteen minutes later the two police officers reached the spot just off Route 8 where Garrow had stashed his car. The VW was cleverly hidden on an abandoned logging road, under a blanket of pine boughs cut from nearby trees. But the sun's reflection off the windshield had revealed the car's hiding place to a passing trooper.

McCabe greeted the two troopers guarding the car, then began examining the vehicle. He carefully unloaded the contents of the car: a flannel sleeping bag, a stock of canned food, several changes of clothing, and various tools. McCabe placed these items into clear plastic bags and handed them to Don Ambler.

"Tag these, and have someone run them down to the lab in Albany," McCabe instructed. "I also want this car torn apart. I want to know the origination of every hair in the carpeting. I don't give a damn if the lab boys have to trace them down as coming from the German workers who assembled this crate."

"I'll have the car towed to the lab in Albany," Ambler said as he passed the bags of evidence to a trooper standing nearby.

McCabe opened the VW's glove box. Inside was a single item, a New York State map. He carefully unfolded the map, tried studying it in the failing light, then said to the trooper standing alongside Major Ambler, "Put your flashlight on this thing, willya?"

The trooper did as requested, and McCabe looked the map over carefully.

Ambler noted the rigid intensity of McCabe's expression. "What have you got?"

"Can't be certain," McCabe answered. Across the map, in various locations around upper New York State, were red dots. Next to several of the dots were names written in red ink. First names. All female. "But if my hunch is right, we might be onto something even bigger than we thought."

Running his index finger down the map, McCabe counted the dots. There were twenty-seven in all.

"Whew!" Ambler gasped. "You don't suppose . . . ?"

"I don't know what the hell to think right now, Don. Except that I want a detail of investigators to check out the locations of these dots against the names. We might be on the verge of clearing up a whole file drawer full of unsolved homicides."

The two men looked at each other for a long moment. "What now?" Ambler finally asked.

McCabe stepped out onto the deserted highway and glanced up at Mount Pleasant. The mountain was a deep gold at the top, where it caught the last of the dying sunlight.

"He's up there somewhere," McCabe said, "and we're going to search every square foot of those woods until we find that bastard. And I want to take him alive, Don. Pass the word to your men that there's to be no shooting unless they're caught in a life-threatening situation. I want to find out where he's got that Petz girl—and God knows who else—stashed. Before it's too late."

"So it's stale sandwiches, soggy sleeping bags, and lots of insect repellent," Ambler offered from behind a weak smile.

"Afraid so," McCabe added. His eyes were still trained on the mountain looming over the highway. It was as if he were issuing a private challenge to Garrow.

The BCI investigator considered the one detail of evidence in the Domblewski and Porter murders that he had carefully shielded from the press: the indication of the killer's style the police would use to eliminate any bogus confessions from unbalanced publicity seekers certain to step forward in a sensational case such as this. Domblewski and Porter had each been stabbed several times around the heart. The neat, exacting, shallow incisions were meant not to kill, but to torture. McCabe had been infuriated by Garrow's calculated cruelty. This wasn't a man who murdered simply out of passion, but one who did so in a cold-blooded, ruthless, and punishing manner.

Before he climbed back into his car, McCabe called to Don Ambler. "I want an elbow-to-elbow cordon along this highway, all around that mountain."

"Elbow-to-elbow! Where the hell do I get that many men?"

"I don't care. Just get them. I don't give a damn if you have to cancel every trooper's vacation to do it. But I don't want Garrow to make it across this highway. He gets off that mountain, he's got six million acres of mostly uninhabited wilderness in which to hide. Don, that's an area about the size of the states of Vermont and New Hampshire combined."

Ambler let himself heavily into the passenger seat of McCabe's car. "Only way he's going to get over this highway, Henry, is to feel his way across. He dropped his glasses near Domblewski's body. They're so strong you can start fires with them."

"One for our side," McCabe answered and twisted the ignition key. "And I got the feeling we're going to need all the breaks we can get on this one."

Less than a mile away and about halfway up Mount Pleasant, Robert Garrow waited quietly. He had been in this wooded spot for over an hour, staying put until darkness came. Garrow understood that when night fell the searchers would withdraw from the woods to secure Route 8, and they would wait until morning to resume the manhunt. With the searchers out of the forest, he would move to another point on the mountain and sit out the following day. That the state troopers had him hemmed in with their cordon along Route 8, the only road out of the area, didn't overly concern him. He could escape detection simply by staying in the woods and avoiding the open meadow areas.

As daylight expired, the mosquitoes and deer flies came out in full force. A swarm of blood-sucking insects began feasting on Garrow, raising welts on his face, hands, and neck. When he could stand it no longer, he pushed himself to his feet and slung his rifle and backpack over his shoulder. Holding his hands in front of his face to protect his eyes from the branches he could barely make out because of the darkness and because of his poor vision, he made his way slowly up the mountain.

He had gone about fifty yards, constantly slapping at his

face to kill the biting insects, when he heard the rippling of one of the countless streams veining the mountain. Garrow followed the sound. Breaking out of the underbrush, he nearly stepped into the swift, black water. He bent and scooped up a handful of mud from along the bank of the stream, and caked his face, neck, and balding head with cold mud as protection against the mosquitoes and deer flies. That done, he continued up the mountain, following the course of the stream. To be certain he couldn't be tracked by police dogs, he crossed the shallow stream several times.

After traveling a couple of hundred yards he came upon a crudely constructed wooden bridge. There he left the stream bank and began walking along the grass and dirt road that traversed the mountain incline.

He began to feel chilled. Though the temperature had dropped only slightly and was still in the sixties, Garrow's clothes were wet from crossing the stream, and the night air easily penetrated his red cotton shirt and khaki pants. He glanced up at the moonless sky, grateful at least that it was clear. Rain in these mountains, even in the summer, was punishingly cold to an improperly dressed man.

He nearly walked by a dark, boxlike structure just off the road without noticing it. A cabin. Garrow checked the area for cars. None around. Then, aware that anyone inside the cabin might see him approaching, he walked along the tree line. He moved on his toes up the front steps and across the porch and peeked through the curtainless window. The place looked empty. He knocked lightly on the door. Getting no response, he tried the knob. It was locked.

Garrow took a half step back and threw his shoulder against the door. There was a muted, crunching sound as the lockset tore loose from the doorjamb. He let himself in and struck a match. The one-room hunting cabin contained a small wood stove and four cots placed along the walls. Off to one corner was an icebox and cooking stove and a deep-well, slop sink. Over the sink were some shelves stocked with a few canned goods. Garrow put the cans into his backpack, then struck another match. He checked out the pegs protruding from the front wall. No coats or jackets. He opened the drawers of the small dresser, in which he found a green sweatshirt and plum-colored moleskin slacks that were considerably heavier than his khaki pants. He peeled off his wet clothes and tried on the sweatshirt and moleskins. They fit perfectly, and his face split into an unseen smile. He considered leaving his clothes in the drawer but thought better of it, as he did the idea of laying up for the night in the cabin. The troopers would search these cabins right off. Caught in here, he would have no place to run.

Garrow left the cabin and followed the road back to the stream. Careful to remain dry, he traced the stream about another half mile farther up the mountain, then cut into the woods. He stumbled across a large rotting log. Quickly cutting some pine boughs from nearby trees with the ax from his backpack, he made a bed there for himself. He covered himself with pine branches and was satisfied that the searchers would have to stumble over him to find him. He fell asleep with his arm around his hunting rifle.

Three days later, at the new command post at the foot of Mount Pleasant, Henry McCabe was awakened in his bunk in one of the state police mobile sleeper trucks by a uniformed trooper.

"Phone call for you, sir," the uniformed officer announced, poking McCabe's shoulder.

"Huh? What the hell?" McCabe answered. One eye was still plastered closed with sleep.

"This way, sir," the young officer directed.

"I know where the damned phone trailer is," McCabe growled. He pushed himself from the hinged bunk, twisted his fatigues so they fit him like they were supposed to, then walked around to the side of the sleeper truck. Looking around at the cool clear morning while he urinated on the rear tire, McCabe added, "Give me a little hot weather, or some rain maybe, will-ya, God? Just so that bastard ain't so bloody comfortable in those woods. Make it tough on him, please, God."

The smiling trooper led McCabe to the phone trailer. Major Don Ambler was standing near the portable switchboard, sipping coffee. He rolled his eyes when McCabe reached for the phone.

"Yeah?" McCabe barked into the mouthpiece. When after a pause he continued more respectfully, Ambler's face lit up with a knowing grin. "Ah yes, governor," McCabe explained into the phone. "I feel we have him trapped within a ten-mile square. We've made contact with the suspect a couple of times. Once Garrow practically ran into one of our officers, but he slipped back into the woods before we could apprehend him."

McCabe listened to the governor, then answered, "I realize that the merchants in this area are screaming that this thing has closed down the Adirondack tourist trade. But we just can't allow people into this area. Gawkers interfere with our operations, and campers are in danger from Garrow. . . . Yes, governor, I understand that this search is costing the taxpayers over fifty thousand dollars a day, but we're doing our best. We're out in the bush from sunup until nine o'clock every night. These woods are so thick you can't even see a man walking five feet off your flank. And Garrow has thousands of square miles of that kind of terrain in which to hide. . . .

"What you may not understand, governor, is the level of fear gripping this area. Everyone is armed; even housewives and kids are carrying weapons. People are so paranoid we're getting reports of Garrow being sighted all over the northern part of the state—reports we have to check out."

McCabe paused again.

"Thank you, sir. We'll keep pressing him. Goodbye, governor."

McCabe hung up the phone. Ambler handed him a cup of coffee. The BCI investigator took a deep sip, then waited, as if to allow the coffee to prime his heart for full action. He turned to Ambler and with guarded cynicism said, "With only forty-seven hundred people in this entire county, chances are the governor didn't spend much time campaigning around here; he has no idea what kind of conditions we're facing. He thinks all we have to do is sweep our men across something like Central Park and pick Garrow up. He should see how our guys are getting torn up by the underbrush, how they are getting eaten alive by the bugs."

Ambler nodded his agreement, then stepped to a spot in front of the topographic map of Hamilton County tacked on the wall. He pointed to a quadrant on the north side of Mount Pleasant, near Long Lake and some ten miles from the command post. "We put the dog squads out at six. They're working this area."

"Anything yet?" McCabe asked. He downed his coffee.

"Nothing," Ambler answered.

With that McCabe stalked out of the communications trailer and headed for the sleeper truck. This thing was starting to get to him. The manhunt was turning into a personal challenge; he didn't like being made a fool of by anyone. It was bad enough that the local people and practically the entire New York State media establishment, were on his back to apprehend Garrow; now the governor was leaning on him. Beyond that, McCabe had another reason for nailing Garrow as soon as possible. All the evidence pointed to Garrow as having abducted Susan Petz. If he hadn't killed her and had her stashed in these woods, time was running out for the girl. McCabe wanted to believe that Susan Petz was still alive. He wanted to believe that if he could apprehend Garrow, he might be able to get out of the fugitive where he had hidden the girl.

Once back at the sleeper truck, McCabe reached under his bunk for his boots. As he slipped them on, he thought, Maybe this will be the day we'll get lucky.

Approximately thirteen hours later Robert Garrow peered out from a tangle of impenetrable underbrush. He had been in this same area all day—near Route 8 and about three miles from Speculator—content to stay put and monitor hourly newscasts of the manhunt on his pocket radio. The news had been full of reports about the troopers' finding Garrow's red shirt and khaki pants under a rotted log near the summit of Mount Pleasant. Also broadcast repeatedly that day was the replay of the television plea his attorney, Frank Armani, had made: "Running away will do you no good, Robert. I'm willing to help. Come on in, and you won't get hurt."

Garrow had had a good laugh at Armani's assurance that he wouldn't be harmed if he gave himself up. Lawyers should spend a little time behind bars, he had mused, so that they would understand what happened to men who did time for molesting or raping children. A man convicted of these crimes was considered the lowest form of human life by the rest of the prison population. He caught the full effect of the furious, helpless guilt suffered by inmates who had children on the outside, children they were powerless to protect or care for. While locked up in the early sixties, Garrow had seen one convicted child molester get his eyes dug out with a butter knife.

Garrow sat very still and waited patiently for darkness. He

was following the same plan that he had used to elude capture for the past four days: Wait to see what moves the searchers made, listen for their dogs, and change locations only if forced to. At night he found a safe place to sleep and so regained his strength for the following day.

Garrow knew that if he kept his stamina, his chances of remaining free were good. To do that, in addition to restoring himself with sleep, he needed food. The tension of being hunted and the rigorous work of fighting through the thick forest had given him a voracious appetite. He had quickly consumed the canned goods he had stolen from the hunting cabin. For the past two days, he had subsisted on skunk cabbage and berries. The day before yesterday he had captured a ground snake and, not wishing to chance someone spotting smoke from a fire, had eaten the snake raw. But now Garrow realized that he had to break out of the police net to build himself up with proper food. He would get his energy back and head for Canada. He spoke French and could easily lose himself in a city the size of Montreal. Once there, he would send for his family.

It was while thinking about how it might be to live in Canada with his family that he heard the helicopter approach. Even before he caught sight of the aircraft, Garrow knew by the rotor's distinctive *blat-blat-blat* that it was a jet-powered model. The helicopter began turning large circles overhead, and an amplified voice droned down over the wilderness. It was a voice Garrow recognized immediately, and it caused his heart to thump against his chest.

"Honey, this is Edith. Won't you please come out? Leave your rifle in the woods. I am here with the state police. They do not want to hurt you, and they don't want you to hurt anyone else. The children and I want you to come out. Please listen to me and do what I ask."

His gaze fixed skyward, Robert Garrow's eyes filled with tears as he thought of his wife in the helicopter. Then another voice echoed over the silent woodlands.

"This is Robert, Dad. I'm here with Mom. Won't you please listen to us and come out in the open? We don't want you to get hurt. *Please* come out."

When their pleas were repeated verbatim, over and over, Garrow realized that his wife and son were not actually riding in the helicopter. Their messages had been recorded. The helicopter headed west, and the voices grew fainter until he could no longer hear them.

Once it was sufficiently dark, Garrow left his hiding place. He slipped silently amid the trees parallel to Route 8, out of sight of any passing motorists, and walked toward Speculator. When he reached a large outcropping of rock overlooking the road, he turned into the woods. Twenty yards from the highway and shelved neatly into the hillside and obscured by foliage was the lean-to he had constructed two days earlier. He had done such a masterful job of camouflaging the three-by-six-foot hut that he nearly walked right by it himself.

Placing his gun down beside him, Garrow nestled comfortably into the pine boughs he had fashioned for a bed. Once settled, he was able to hear the voices of troopers. He smiled to think of how furious the police would be if they knew that their quarry was camping within a stone's throw of their command post. Garrow's logic in constructing the lean-to where he had was masterful. He knew the police would never think to scour the area right around their search headquarters. They would never figure him to be hiding right under their noses. Situated there, each night Garrow was amused to hear the searchers curse him loudly for his elusiveness. Listening to them, even he was beginning to believe he was some kind of phantom.

After resting about an hour, Garrow decided to chance a closer look. He moved stealthily through the underbrush to a spot where he could see into the command post. Dozens of uniformed men milled about the area. One trooper even walked to within three feet of him to relieve himself in the bushes. Garrow was tempted to reach out and take the trooper's hat as protection against the night chill.

After the officer returned to the compound, Garrow fixed his attention on the helicopter parked in the clearing next to the command post. Garrow had worked on helicopters as an Air Force mechanic. Because he knew enough about the aircraft to fly it, he considered stealing it, but he nixed the idea after remembering that jet-powered helicopters required a few minutes warm-up time before they would fly. The troopers would nail him before he could get off the ground.

Just then the skies opened up with one of those flash summer thunderstorms common in the Adirondacks. For about ten minutes the rain came down sideways in sheets. Then, as quickly as it had begun, the storm subsided. When the wind and rain stopped, Garrow heard someone calling orders to the troopers stationed along Route 8. Garrow recognized Henry McCabe's voice from the news broadcasts about the manhunt he had monitored.

"Everyone okay out there?" the BCI investigator asked through a hand-held bullhorn.

There were communal grumbles from the nearby highway.

"Shine that searchlight on the road, willya?" McCabe ordered.

The big light flicked on and panned the highway. As far as Garrow could see was a line of stark-naked state troopers. Some were wringing out their clothes; others dumped water out of their boots. Most were cursing loudly. The fugitive chuckled. He considered taking advantage of the confusion to make a break across the highway. How would it look when the media reported that Robert Garrow had broken out of the police dragnet while scores of troopers stood naked on the highway, unable to give chase because they didn't have their pants or boots on? But Garrow decided against trying it; he had a better plan.

Four nights later, about an hour before dawn, he slipped undetected into the parking lot of Deer Foot Lodge. Located near Speculator on Lake Pleasant, Deer Foot Lodge, like other Adirondack vacation resorts, had been financially devastated by the Domblewski murder and by the subsequent manhunt. About the only patrons who hadn't canceled their reservations were out-of-staters who had decided against turning right around and driving hundreds of miles back home. Most of these out-of-staters believed they were safe in the larger resorts such as Deer Foot Lodge.

Garrow moved quietly through the parking lot, peering into car windows until he found what he was looking for. A white 1973 Pontiac with Ohio plates had the keys in the ignition. Keeping his eyes on the nearby darkened lodge, Garrow opened the car door softly and slipped in behind the wheel. He turned the key, and the engine growled into life. Careful because of his bad eyesight, he drove slowly out of the resort compound.

Once out on the highway, he noticed something on the dashboard, a glasses case. He said a quick prayer as he removed a pair of round, gold wire-rimmed glasses from the case and tried them on. The fuzziness disappeared from his vision. Garrow wanted to shout with happiness. Next he glanced back and saw what resembled a hatbox on the back seat. He turned and grabbed it. Inside was a woman's wig, blond with long curls. He put it on, glanced in the rearview mirror, and smiled. Not Marilyn Monroe, but it might buy him a few precious seconds, he thought as he took the wig off.

Driving tentatively along the deserted highway, he checked the gas gauge. The red needle was riding between a quarter full and empty. He would have to get gas at some point, but not now. There was enough for his immediate purposes.

Garrow drove along the quiet streets of the mountain village of Speculator, then turned north on Route 30. From news reports he had monitored while in the woods, he knew the roadblock was located about five miles from town. He also guessed that, after being up all night, the troopers manning the roadblock wouldn't be totally alert; they would be waiting for their relief so they could get back to the command post for some sleep. If he got by the roadblock, it was clear sailing. There were no towns along Route 30 for twenty or so miles, until Sabael near Indian Lake. If his gas held out, he had a chance.

Daylight had backlit the mountains in orange by the time he approached the two trooper cars parked in a *V* pattern across the highway with just enough room between them for a car to pass through. Steering with one hand and maintaining the Pontiac's speed at thirty miles per hour, Garrow slipped on the blond wig. About a hundred yards from the roadblock, close enough so he could see both troopers dozing in one of the cars, Garrow put the pedal to the floor. The Pontiac seemed to lift from the road as it accelerated to eighty. Garrow lined up the groove in the hood with the yellow line, closed his eyes, and flew between the trooper cars with only inches to spare. He had already traveled several hundred yards before he saw one of the police cars peel out after him.

A wild chase ensued over the next several miles. Both vehicles screamed along the quiet country road in excess of a hundred miles per hour, with the police car matching the Pontiac's speed on the turns and gaining on the straightaways. The blue and yellow car pulled to within a half mile of him, and Garrow briefly considered crashing into the woods. If he didn't get hurt, he could try to escape on foot. Before he could act on that thought, as he rapidly alternated his gaze between the road and the rearview mirror, Garrow noticed blue smoke belching out of the police car's grill. The pursuing car slowed and pulled off the road. Garrow felt a sense of elation. Their engine had seized. Must have broken a fan belt.

Forty miles up Route 30, near Horseshoe Lake, Garrow pulled off on a logging road. He would wait out the daylight hours, then continue north after dark. To escape detection from the air, he cut branches from nearby trees and lay them over the car. Satisfied the Pontiac was well camouflaged, he made his way into the woods and found a high spot of ground where he could watch both the road and the car.

Around nine that evening, after sleeping most of the day, Garrow uncovered the car, got in, and headed up Route 30. About an hour up the road he tensed when he spotted car lights coming up fast behind him. Quickly slipping on the blond wig, he cut the Pontiac's speed to forty. If it was a state police car, he figured, they would expect him to attempt to outrun them again. He would chance that the troopers who'd chased him the previous morning hadn't gotten close enough to get the make of the Pontiac. If he drove innocently and wore the wig, they might mistake him for a woman and whip right by him.

The approaching car nearly rear-ended the Pontiac before swerving around it at the last moment. As he flew by, the driver of the black Cadillac glanced irritatedly at Garrow for a flashing second. The man in the Cadillac had neatly combed gray hair, a matching mustache, and a lean, long face. It was a face Robert Garrow would see again. It belonged to George Marthen, district judge for the northern New York region. He was on his way to hear a case the following morning in St. Lawrence County.

During the following thirty minutes of driving along the country road, Garrow enjoyed a rare sense of relief. By breaking out of the police dragnet, he had changed the rules of the search. No longer were the troopers looking for a needle in a haystack. Now they would have to locate that same needle in any of a hundred haystacks.

But Garrow made a mistake that surprised his searchers, including the highly incensed Henry McCabe. Instead of heading due north, where he could cross the Canadian border at any number of places by foot or by car, he doubled back along Route 30 and turned east on Route 28. Inexplicably, he made for his sister Agnes Mandy's house in Witherbee, some eighty miles from the site of the Domblewski killing and near the Vermont border.

Garrow was identified when he stopped for gas in North Creek, giving BCI Investigator McCabe a hint as to his destination. McCabe's hunch was confirmed after Garrow slipped by the police guard in front of his sister's house in Witherbee and used her tapped phone to call his wife in Syracuse. Once McCabe received the information about Garrow's phone call, he ordered several dozen troopers and conservation officers to dress as loggers, fishermen, and tourists and to move into the Witherbee area. On August 9th, eleven days after the Domblewski murder, an undercover trooper staked out near Agnes Mandy's house spotted David, Garrow's sixteen-year-old nephew, carrying food into the woods adjacent to the Mandy house. Within minutes troopers and conservation officers closed in and flushed Garrow out of the woods into a watch line of other armed officers.

When Garrow saw the column of men along the road in front of him, he cut to his right and began running wildly in zig-zag fashion toward the trees. Closest to Garrow was Henry LaBlanc, a conservation officer. Realizing that if Garrow made it to the woods he stood a good chance of eluding his searchers, LaBlanc, despite orders to take the fugitive alive if at all possible, opened fire with his high-powered rifle.

Garrow lurched forward as the deer slugs tore into his back, arm, and leg and was knocked off-stride. But even though seriously wounded and bleeding heavily, he recovered his footing and ran another hundred yards. He had just made it to the tree line when LaBlanc's second volley of gunfire nearly tore his left foot off. The force of the slugs blew Garrow's leg out from under him, and he flipped into the brush like a rag doll and fell unconscious.

The largest manhunt in the history of New York State had come to an end. The man wanted for murdering Philip Domblewski, and the prime suspect in over half a dozen other homicides throughout New York State, was in custody.

As news of Garrow's capture spread, the inhabitants of the Adirondack region fell into a relieved, jubilant mood. Hand-painted signs expressing gratitude to the state troopers for apprehending Robert Garrow appeared along highways throughout northern New York.

4

August 9, 1973

Frank Armani, napkin stuck in his collar to shield his white shirt and burgundy tie from food splashings, had just settled down to dinner with his wife, Mary, and two daughters. Twenty-year-old Debbie and sixteen-year-old Dorina, both dark-eyed, dark-haired, and pale-skinned, sat on each side of their father at the table. The phone rang. Armani looked up from his plate of calamari.

"I'll get it," Mary Armani said. She waved her husband down and pushed away from the table. "If you're going to make it to Utica by seven-thirty, you'd better eat."

Armani absentmindedly watched his wife move through the dining alcove to the sunken living room, where the phone was jangling. Though she could easily pass for Italian, Mary was full-blooded Spanish. She had wavy brown hair, green eyes, and a round calm face dominated by full lips and high cheekbones. She gave off an air of well-groomed, expensively dressed homeyness. Mary was the kind of woman to whom men went for counsel rather than an affair. Mary and Frank had been sweethearts since they had attended Solvay High School in Syracuse together. They were married while Armani was studying at Syracuse University.

Armani turned his attention back to his dinner, took a couple of generous bites, then glanced up at his wife. Her expression turned darkly serious as she placed the phone down on the credenza.

"What is it?" Armani called.

"It's Edith Garrow," his wife answered, as she walked back to the dinner table. "They've captured her husband. He's been shot and is in very critical condition."

Armani yanked the napkin from his shirt collar, shoved away from the table, and hurried across the living room to the phone.

"Where are you calling from, Edith?" he asked quickly.

In a tear-choked, near-hysterical voice, Edith Garrow explained that she had been brought north in a state police helicopter after being advised that her husband had been rushed to Champlain Valley Physicians Hospital in Plattsburgh. Robert was presently in surgery; it was still uncertain if he would survive his injuries.

"I arrived here just before they took him into surgery," the woman explained. "He asked me to call you. He wants you to represent him, Mr. Armani."

"I'll have to speak with him about that," Armani hedged. He wanted to be certain he could handle the job before accepting it.

"He won't talk with anyone but you about the Domblewski murder or the Porter—"

"Hold it, Edith," Armani interrupted sharply. "I don't want you to say anything else about this matter over the phone. Wait until I get up there, and you and I will discuss it in person. Further, you're not to talk with anyone else until I get there. Do you understand? Not to the police, news reporters, your relatives, or friends—*anyone.*"

"An Investigator McCabe has already asked me a lot of questions," the woman offered.

"Damn him," Armani muttered. McCabe had promised to call him the minute they captured Garrow.

"McCabe wanted to know where Robert was on certain days in June. Days he missed work—"

"Please, Edith," the lawyer cut in. "Wait until I get up there. You can't tell about these phones."

Armani had good reason to suspect that the BCI was keeping close tabs on Edith Garrow. When the woman had visited Armani's office during the manhunt, he had spotted an unmarked state police car in the gas station across the street. The car had tailed Edith Garrow's taxi after she had left his office. Further, for the past ten days, Armani had noticed a similar car driven by a lone male occupant following him. So badly did the state police want information and clues on the Daniel Porter murder, Susan Petz disappearance, and on the other unsolved murders for which Robert Garrow was the prime suspect that Armani didn't put it past them to ignore a few people's civil rights and tap a phone or two.

"Do you know if Robert told them anything?" Armani asked.

"McCabe claimed that my husband wouldn't talk to him; all he did was ask to see you," the woman replied.

"Good," Armani added. He hoped McCabe had told her the truth.

"Okay, Edith. I want you to call me tomorrow after Robert has been out of surgery for a while and let me know how he's doing. No sense me coming up there until your husband can talk."

He hung up the phone and returned to the table, where his wife and daughters were silently picking at their food.

The lawyer took a few bites, then leaned away from the table.

"I thought you were hungry," Mary said.

"I was," Armani answered.

"Coffee?" She got up from the table and took her husband's plate.

"Yeah, please," he answered. Armani was lost in thought, his eyes glazed over.

When Mary returned to the table with his cup of coffee, she asked, "Why do you have to do it, Frank? Why do you have to be the one who takes this case?"

"I haven't officially taken his case yet, Mary," he answered, slightly irritated. It irked him to have his wife prying into his business. "I'm just going up there at Garrow's request. I owe that to him as a client."

"I'm worried about this thing," Mary persisted. "You've never defended a man charged with murder. Isn't it out of your league?"

"What's *that* supposed to mean?" Armani's irritation gave

way to hurt feelings. Though Mary meant well and had his interests at heart, sometimes she expressed things in a manner that seemed condescending to her husband's personal and professional abilities, as though he were a little kid.

"Your practice is mostly liability work. You don't do much criminal work."

"First of all, Mary," Armani explained petulantly, "Garrow doesn't have the money to pay a private attorney; he'll probably be assigned a public defender. Chances are the court wouldn't even appoint me, because, as you've mentioned, I don't do much criminal work and have never defended a murder suspect . . . although, as you remember, I did prosecute a couple of homicides when I was with the DA's office. So don't worry about it. I don't really want the damned case. It'll just be a lot of work, and a king-sized pain in the keister. I'm only going up to Plattsburgh because right now Garrow won't talk to anyone else. He deserves at least that much."

"I just don't like the thing. I wish you'd stay away from it altogether," Mary finished.

Debbie looked up from her food. "You've already said that, Mom."

A frustrated Mary Armani took to gathering the dishes. That was how it always went with her family—Frank got bullheaded about something, and the girls took his side. But Mary was the one who had to listen to her husband complain when he was overworked or when he got burned on a case by not getting paid for his time.

5

August 10, 1973

Edith Garrow phoned Armani from the hospital to advise the lawyer that her husband had survived his surgery and was recovering from his gunshot wounds. He was able to talk and was asking for Armani.

That evening Armani made the five-hour drive to Plattsburgh. Once at Champlain Valley Physicians Hospital and after a brief, inconclusive discussion with timid, introverted, and frightened Edith Garrow, he was shown past the detail of troopers sealing off the fifth floor and let into Robert Garrow's room.

Garrow sat propped up in bed, staring blankly at one wall of his dimly lit room. His left arm and left foot were in a cast.

"How are you feeling, Bob?" the lawyer asked, taking the chair next to the bed.

"Lots of pain," Robert Garrow answered. He pushed his glasses up on his chalky face with his good hand and winced at the effort.

"They treating you okay?"

"No, Frank, they ain't."

"What do you mean?"

"They started when I was in the ambulance on the way up here," Garrow began, nearly whining. "They kept asking me about some girl."

42

"The Petz girl?"

"Yeah, that's the one, Frank. When I couldn't tell them anything, they twisted my arm and foot until I passed out. They slapped me around until I woke up, then started with the questions again."

Armani nodded and wrote something on his notepad.

"When I got here, the doctors refused to treat me until I talked to the cops. I kept trying to tell them I didn't know anything about any Petz girl. I guess the doctor finally convinced the troopers that I'd die unless they took me upstairs to surgery."

"How they been treating you since you've been out of surgery?"

"Been in here solid asking me more questions since I been conscious, Frank. Plus that trooper on the door keeps coming in and taking my food and water."

"I'll check into it and see that you're not bothered anymore," Armani answered.

"Frank, you gotta help me," Garrow blurted, tears filling his eyes.

"It's not quite that simple," Armani answered, bothered slightly by Garrow's addressing him by his first name so often. "Your defense is going to cost quite a bit of money to prepare. You don't have that kind of dough, so the court will appoint you a public defender, someone who will be quite capable of handling your case."

"I don't want any other lawyer. I want you to represent me, Frank," Garrow pleaded. "Take everything I've got. But please, Frank, you gotta stay with me on this one."

Garrow was pathetic. The once awesome, forbidding man had been transformed into a shrunken, crying hulk. Armani caught himself feeling sorry for him . . . and then remembered what he was charged with.

"I'm not sure it can be worked out," Armani hedged. "I'll see what I can do and be back sometime tomorrow to see you. In the meantime, you're not to talk with *anyone,* including your wife. Someone wants to talk with you, refer them to me. You hear?"

"I won't say a word to anyone," Garrow answered.

Armani stood. He was about to leave the room when a tearful Garrow called to him. "I'm begging you, Frank. You're my only chance. You know me good. You're on my side. I don't stand a snowball's chance in hell with a public defender. Please stand by me, Frank."

"Let me try and work it out," Armani answered, genuinely affected by Garrow's plea.

He left Garrow's room and stepped to the pay phone down the hall. He placed a call to Judge George Marthen in Lake Pleasant. Marthen, as the district judge, was certain to try the Garrow case. Marthen agreed to see Armani first thing in the morning and gave the lawyer directions to his house.

Armani rode the elevator to the ground floor. He was heading out of the hospital when he was stopped by a uniformed trooper. The officer led Armani to a small visiting room off the main lobby, where an exhausted-looking Henry McCabe waited. The BCI investigator handed Armani a cup of vending machine coffee.

"I like the way you called me when you apprehended Garrow," Armani challenged.

"Things got hectic up here. Sorry," McCabe answered.

"What's this about my client being tortured in the ambulance on the way to the hospital? And what about the doctors refusing to treat him until he told you what you wanted to know? Or how about your troopers harassing him by taking his water and food away?"

"Garrow's full of baloney."

"He's also got some civil rights," Armani countered.

"Nobody's touched him or his food and water. The guy's a crybaby."

"I'm going to check out his allegations, McCabe. If he's right, there's going to be hell to pay."

"Yeah, yeah," the BCI investigator answered, apparently unconcerned by Armani's threat. "All I did was ask him where he stashed the Petz girl."

"You don't know that he took the Petz girl."

"Everything we've got points to your boy abducting Susan Petz . . . after he killed Daniel Porter. I'll do anything I can to get to that girl in time . . . if she's still alive."

"I get your point," Armani replied. "If she's in those woods, I want to find her alive, too."

"Should Garrow talk to you about her whereabouts, let us know, will you? If she's in the woods, she doesn't have much time left. The temperature has been dropping into the forties at night."

"I'll see what I can do," the lawyer finished, feeling heavy with the conflict he faced—the conflict between his duty to his client, and his duty to possibly save a life, and thus prevent the commission of a crime—in this case, murder. "Now I've got to get going."

Armani stood and left the small room. McCabe leaned back in his chair and squeezed the bridge of his nose between his thumb and forefinger. The manhunt had worn him out. The pressure of the past two days' continuous search for Susan Petz had been even more grueling. McCabe was certain Garrow had grabbed the Petz girl, and he meant to find out where he had hidden her.

Armani drove straight to Speculator and spent what was left of the night in Zeiser's, a rustic country inn near Lake Pleasant. Promptly at nine o'clock the following morning, he eased his car into Judge George Marthen's driveway. Elsa Marthen, the judge's tall, robust wife, greeted Armani at the front door.

"He's waiting for you on the porch, Mr. Armani," she said warmly.

She led the lawyer through the neatly kept colonial-style house to the back sun porch. Silver-haired, tall, and lean, George Marthen was seated in an easy chair, staring out at the mirror-calm waters of Lake Pleasant.

"Nice to meet you, Mr. Armani," the judge greeted him, standing to take the lawyer's hand. "Coffee?"

"Sure, black."

Armani studied Marthen while the judge moved to pour him a cup of coffee. He walked lightly on his feet for a man six-feet-four-inches tall, and appeared to be in excellent physical condition. Armani had heard that Marthen was a fair but hard-nosed judge, one who maintained absolute control over his courtroom. Appointed to the bench by Nelson Rockefeller, Marthen openly favored the death penalty and was recognized as a man who didn't coddle habitual offenders.

The judge returned from the kitchen and handed Armani a cup of coffee.

"Thanks," the lawyer said. Gazing out over the lake, he added, "Gorgeous up here."

"Moved to Lake Pleasant ten years ago from Long Island," Marthen said, lighting a cigarette. He tossed the match into a butt-filled ashtray. "Don't know why the hell I waited so long to do it."

"God's country," Armani seconded.

Marthen nodded in reply. "Now, about the Garrow matter."

"As I told you last night on the phone, I've represented him in the past."

"I've been advised that he won't talk with any lawyer but you," Marthen interjected.

"He'll change his mind about that if he has to."

"I'm not so sure, Frank," the judge added. "Let's look at it this way. You know Garrow better than anyone. He trusts you. The way I see it, you can do the best job defending him."

"There're some problems. He has no money to pay for extensive legal fees."

"So I'll appoint you his public defender," Marthen quipped.

"You realize I've never defended a murder suspect before? Closest I've come was prosecuting a couple of homicides as an assistant district attorney."

"I wouldn't worry about it," Marthen counseled. "Good legal principles apply regardless of whether you're prosecuting or defending someone."

Armani leaned back in the wicker chair and stared at the lake. A loon was flying low over the water, its reflection showing clearly on the smooth surface.

"I can sign the papers this morning appointing you his attorney," Marthen prodded. "Garrow *is* entitled to the counsel of his choice, and it *is* the court's responsibility to meet that request . . . if that attorney is available. Does your time allow you to take his case, Frank?"

"Yeah, I can work it in."

"Then it's settled."

"I hope I know what the hell I'm getting into," Armani said, standing.

"Ah, you'll do fine," Marthen said, pushing to his feet. "From everything I've learned about you, you'll put on a great defense for your client."

Not unmindful that he was being flattered, Armani leveled

his gaze at the judge. "Why do I feel like I have no choice in this matter?"

Judge Marthen smiled. "Let's just say that it appears as though you've been appointed by circumstance to defend Mr. Garrow."

6

August 11, 1973

Armani drove directly to Plattsburgh from Judge
Marthen's house. He was at Robert Garrow's bedside by noon,
explaining to the overjoyed murder suspect that he would handle his defense.

"You mind if I tape our sessions, Bob? Saves me from doing
a lot of writing." Armani reached into his briefcase for his portable tape recorder.

"If it'll help you," Garrow said. While Armani set up his
cassette recorder on Garrow's meal tray and tested it to be certain it was functioning properly, the murder suspect asked, "I
wondered if you could do something for me, Frank?"

"What's that?"

"Talk to that trooper guarding my door. He comes in my
room a lot; he sits at the end of my bed and bothers me by
keeping me awake."

"I'll mention it to him. But you have to understand, Bob,
that these troopers are protecting you as well as guarding you.
There are a lot of people out there—nuts—who wouldn't hesi-
tate to come in here and blow you away."

Garrow thought about that one.

"All right," Armani began. "I want you to tell me what
happened at that campground the morning Philip Domblewski
was killed."

"I don't know anything about that, Frank."

"C'mon, Bob. If you want me to help you, you've got to level with me. Are you saying that you weren't there?"

"I was there, but I didn't do anything. I didn't kill anyone."

"Then explain what happened," Armani pressed.

"I stopped by to ask for some gas." Garrow paused, rubbing his forehead with his good hand. "I'm having trouble remembering exactly what happened, Frank."

"You asked the two kids—David Freeman and Carol Ann Malinowski—for gas. Then the other two—Domblewski and Fiorello—showed up." Armani noticed that Garrow was dozing off. "Bob, this is important!"

"Oh, sorry, Frank," Garrow said, his eyes snapping open. "I didn't get any sleep last night. Keep pokin' me so I stay awake, Frank."

"Now tell me what happened when the other two kids showed up."

"They were angry or somethin'. I got scared. Plus I was having one of those headaches."

"Headaches?"

"I get 'em bad, Frank. When I get one, my head feels like it's going to burst. I get 'em here," Garrow explained and ran his hand over the crown of his balding head.

"How long you been having the headaches?"

"For a couple of years, Frank. They hurt terrible. A whole bottle of Excedrins won't even touch the pain."

"You had one of those headaches the morning Domblewski was killed?" Armani repeated for the benefit of the tape recorder.

"Yeah, Frank."

"So what happened at that campground? You said that those two boys were angry and that you were scared. What were you scared about? Did you have an argument or something?"

"Yeah, Frank, that's it. We had an argument."

"About what?"

"They wouldn't give me any gas. Next thing I knew a bunch of men arrived at the campsite," Garrow answered, growing more alert, as if it was all coming back to him. "Keep doing it like that, Frank. Help me remember by asking me questions. I can fill in the details."

"So what happened when those men arrived?"

"I was real scared. I didn't want to go back to prison, Frank. So I ran and ran."

"Hold it. Let's back up a little. You're saying that you didn't kill Philip Domblewski with your knife?"

"I can't remember exactly what happened during the argument, Frank. That's the truth. I was real scared. The headache was so bad. Them cops kept telling me that I killed that kid. But I wouldn't kill anyone, Frank. You know that."

"It doesn't matter what *I* think," Armani said. "We're going to have to convince a jury that you didn't kill the Domblewski kid."

Garrow looked down. "I can't remember, Frank."

"Look, Bob, you're in a hell of a mess," Armani replied, an irritated edge to his voice. "The cops think they've got you cold on the Domblewski murder. You've got to cooperate with me and tell me *everything* that happened that morning at the campsite. You've got to have complete faith in me and not hold anything back. Otherwise they're going to have information that I don't have, and we're going to get slaughtered in that courtroom."

"I want to give you something that'll help you. Honest, Frank. I'm tryin'. Just keep asking me questions."

It went on like that for another seven hours. Robert Garrow claimed he couldn't recall the events preceding Philip Domblewski's death, or the actual death. Armani prodded him repeatedly with bits of information he had gathered about the murder. At eight o'clock that night, the exhausted attorney called it quits. He advised Garrow to call him at his office in Syracuse if he remembered anything more about the morning Philip Domblewski was killed.

7

August 12, 1973

A CLEAR, HOT MORNING. Armani walked along Warren Street in downtown Syracuse, on his way to the Onondaga County courthouse to pick up a copy of the eleven felony counts filed against Robert Garrow as the result of the July incident in which his client had allegedly abducted and sexually molested the two young girls in Geddes. About a block from the Greek revival-style courthouse, Armani ran into an old friend and law colleague, Francis Belge.

"How the hell are you, Frank?" Belge reached for Armani's hand.

"Okay. How about you?" Armani asked, looking his friend over. The last time Armani had seen him, Belge was coming off a bender, and his face had looked as though it had been run through a food processor.

"Sober as a nun," Belge answered. The twinkle in his clear blue eyes, his easy smile, and his clear complexion convinced Armani that his friend was telling the truth.

"I've been wanting to talk with you," Armani added. "Got time for a cup of coffee?"

"All I have time for these days," the six-foot tall, blond-haired Belge kidded.

The two lawyers backtracked a half block to a delicatessen. Once situated at a table and waiting for their order, Armani realized how glad he was to see his friend. He and Belge went

51

back thirty years; they had drunk, skied, and chased women to-gether. Their families were close. The two lawyers had also worked together on several cases over the years, difficult cases in which Armani had needed the aid of a top-flight criminal lawyer. And Francis Belge, now in his mid-forties, was consid-ered by most the best trial lawyer in the area.

So respected was Belge's courtroom talent that over the years local criminal court judges had regularly assigned him the toughest cases. These judges knew that any defendant repre-sented by Francis Belge was guaranteed due process. One of Belge's more famous cases had occurred a couple of years ear-lier, when he had defended Howard Dudley, an itinerant car-nival worker from Syracuse who had left a string of murdered children (including some of his own) and women buried across the country. Belge had prepared an extremely skillful, though unsuccessful defense in the face of a highly inflamed public and press.

The two lawyers were a contrast in looks and background. Belge, trim, handsome, and self-assured, came from an old-line Syracuse family. The short, chunky Armani was the son of im-migrants and hadn't learned English until he was five years old. Armani was more reserved than the flamboyant Belge, a personality difference that had served the two lawyers well in cases on which they had worked as a team. Armani did the me-ticulous research necessary to prepare a client's defense, while Belge handled the courtroom work.

"I've been assigned by Judge Marthen in Hamilton County to act as Robert Garrow's public defender in the Domblewski murder case," Armani began.

"Another lucrative one," Belge kidded. "Why is it, Frank, that we lawyers with social conscience end up in threadbare suits, while the other guys end up with the apartment build-ings?"

"Never knew you to starve, Belge," Armani said and laughed, exhibiting the gap between his upper front teeth. "Garrow is one tough cookie. The son-of-a-bitch plays cat-and-mouse with me when I ask him questions about the Dom-blewski murder. Claims he can't remember anything about it. Says he blacked out, and the next thing he knows half the cops in New York State are chasing him all over the Adirondacks. I have to pin him down to get any information on what occurred in the three days after he was charged with sexually assaulting those two young girls in Geddes. I press him too hard, the guy really gets angry. When he does, I gotta tell you he frightens the hell out of me. His face contorts and turns the color of blood. I want to run out of his hospital room."

"So why did you ever agree to take the case?" Belge sipped his coffee.

"Initially, because he begged me to," Armani answered. "But now I've got a different feeling about this one. I think it's going to be a big case."

Belge listened attentively.

"There's a problem, though. It's stacking up to be a very complicated case. I'm going for an insanity defense—if Garrow can't be proved insane, no one can—so I'll be swamped with doing the research and obtaining the expert testimony. I need someone with balls and savvy to help me."

"Yeah?"

"I'd like you to serve as my co-counsel, Belge."

"No way." The blond lawyer answered without a second's hesitation.

"What's the matter? You too busy?"

"Too sensible," Belge answered. "Garrow doesn't have a prayer of getting a fair trial in the north country. Been too much prejudicial press."

"So we'll get a change of venue."

"You must be joking. Hamilton County hasn't tried a murder case in almost fifty years. They'll never let it go anywhere else. They want to be certain that Garrow hangs for screwing up their number one industry, tourism, for the year."

Armani took time out to drink some coffee.

"Plus Garrow has another strike against him," Belge added.

"And that is?"

"He's got a dumb dago for a lawyer."

"What's that supposed to mean?" Armani bristled.

"Why the hell did you ever agree to go on television during the manhunt and plead for him to give himself up?"

"What was wrong with that?" an irritated Armani asked. "I just told him that he wasn't doing himself any good by running."

Belge leaned over the small table and drilled his friend as though Armani were on the witness stand. "I *know* what the hell you said. It was a grandstand play and one that was tantamount to admitting your client's guilt."

Belge understood how easily the public could be prejudiced to believe a person guilty, how Armani's appearing on television to ask Garrow to give himself up could have been construed as conceding that the suspect had committed a crime.

"You're the last one I thought would put me down for asking my client to come in," Armani countered, the hurt showing in his face. "You, more than anyone, should understand why I asked Garrow to give himself up—that since Garrow was wanted for the Domblewski murder, it was my *obligation* to attempt to convince him to surrender so he could be processed by the judicial system. We do, after all, operate within a system which presumes a person innocent until proven guilty."

"You just try and find a jury in Hamilton County that presumes Garrow to be innocent," Belge answered, a knowing smile on his lips.

"So, am I to take it that, even though this case is right down your alley, you don't want to come in on it with me?"

"Your assumption is correct," Belge finished, pushing back from the table. "I gotta go. Good luck, Armani."

Deeply disappointed, Armani watched Belge stride out of the restaurant. As a result of Belge's turning him down, the feeling of inadequacy that had begun as a premonition during Armani's interviews with Garrow in the Plattsburgh hospital intensified. Armani suspected that he had overcommitted himself on this one. His inability to say no to Garrow or to Judge Marthen had left him up to his neck in a swamp full of crocodiles. Feeling alone and highly vulnerable, he paid the check and left the delicatessen. Up to now he had always been able to count on Francis Belge's help when he needed it.

8

Last Two Weeks of August 1973

Convinced that Garrow had killed Philip Domblewski and that the suspect's only chance was to plead innocent by reason of insanity, Armani began the arduous process of preparing his client's defense. He hoped to establish a lifelong pattern of aberrant behavior in Robert Garrow, so that Judge Marthen would rule at the pretrial insanity hearing that his client was mentally unfit to stand trial. If that failed and Marthen ruled Garrow competent to stand trial, Armani would have to persuade a jury that his client was deranged to the degree that he didn't comprehend the nature or consequences of his crime. Armani would be forced to build an airtight defense around Garrow's being a sick man rather than the cold-blooded killer the prosecution would attempt to prove him to be. To achieve that end, Armani needed to interview Garrow's family and acquaintances, then gather unshakable professional opinions from a battery of psychiatrists.

On the surface Armani found Robert Garrow to be a model husband and family man. He provided well for his wife and two children, Michelle, fifteen, and Robert, fourteen. He was also well-liked in his neighborhood. In the five years the Garrow family had resided on Berwyn Avenue in Syracuse, the murder suspect had repeatedly helped his neighbors dig their cars out of the snow, repair their broken-down appliances, or carry heavy furniture when they moved. On various occasions he had even sponsored fishing and camping trips for neighborhood youngsters. While interviewing Garrow's neighbors, Armani heard a recurrent theme: "We can't believe he would do such a terrible thing. He was so well-liked and thoughtful."

Garrow received similarly high marks from his employer, Millbrook Bakery, where he worked as a master mechanic. Garrow was an almost compulsively hard worker, one who never refused a request to work overtime. There were occasions when Garrow toiled two, even three straight eight-hour shifts. Though not particularly liked by his fellow workers because of his demanding work pace and refusal to socialize with any of them for an after-work beer at a nearby tavern, Garrow was seen as more distant than uncongenial. He was known as a strong patriot who, when pressed, espoused conservative beliefs. He was contemptuous of draft dodgers, welfare recipients, liberals, and hippies. A strong believer in God, he didn't swear or smoke.

As Frank Armani dug deeper, beginning with exhaustive interviews with Edith Garrow, he began to see a shadowed, secret side of Robert Garrow. From Garrow's wife Armani learned that her husband had no close friends, trusted no one. Having formed no real partnership with another human being, including his wife, the murder suspect had no one to whom he could pour out his heart, even if he wanted to. Garrow was also extremely possessive of his wife. He had so isolated the insecure, pliant Edith that she didn't know the names of the people living on either side of her.

The product of a poor farming family from Lowville, New York, Edith Garrow had stood faithfully by her husband during his 1961 arrest and trial in Albany for rape and assault. She had waited for him the eight years he spent in prison. She had served him totally during the years since he had been out of jail. For example, after he had lost his driver's license in 1973 because of a minor parole violation, Edith had walked the several miles round trip each day to Millbrook Bakery to bring him his lunch. She rarely questioned her husband's comings and goings. There had been days on end that past summer when he was missing from their house, absences that coincided with the Domblewski killing, and with Daniel Porter's homicide and Susan Petz's disappearance. Garrow explained away the absences by saying that he had been camping or visiting relatives in northern New York. Further, Edith had lied to Robert's parole officer when the latter questioned her about her husband's failure to report for his regularly scheduled visit in July.

From Edith Garrow, Armani learned more about her husband's headaches. When stricken, Garrow became sexually frenzied and wouldn't leave his wife alone for days at a time; he'd want to make love continuously.

During his interviews with Garrow's children, Armani found that Garrow had passed his penchant for violence to his son. Young Robert had a record of fighting in school and on the streets and carried a knife most of the time.

The real breakthrough in constructing Garrow's insanity defense came when Armani talked with Garrow's two older sisters. Florence Brooks and Agnes Mandy gave Armani a chilling portrait of Robert's childhood. The senior Garrows, Robert and Margaret, were of French-Canadian extraction. In the late 1930s they had settled in the one-bedroom house they still occupied in Mineville, some two hundred yards from the Republic Steel Iron Mine in which the senior Garrow worked. The couple had had seven children, one of whom died in infancy. Another, the eldest boy, had been given away when he was two years old, and his current whereabouts were unknown.

Iron mining was tough, dirty work, and the senior Garrow took to drinking heavily. A strapping man who turned mean when drunk, he vented the brunt of his alcoholic rages on Robert, the oldest boy in the house. The senior Garrow verbally and physically abused young Robert. Sometimes he made the boy kneel facing the wall in the corner for hours at a time as punishment for some minor offense.

Some youngsters escape the full cruelty of one parent by receiving extra love from the second parent. This was not so for Robert Garrow. Five-foot-five-inch, 280-pound Margaret Garrow was a brutal woman, even without the benefit of alcohol. She had a mouth that spewed obscenities, and she took delight in scaring off friends Robert brought home. She ridiculed her son and constantly told him that he was a bad boy and would never amount to anything. She degraded him by forcing him to wear his sisters' old-fashioned tight bloomers out to play. On occasion Margaret stole money from her husband while he was passed out from drinking. When he discovered the theft, the woman blamed young Robert, who then received a beating from both parents.

Beatings were a regular occurrence during young Robert's childhood. Sometimes his punishment was meted out with the buckle end of a wide leather belt. Other times his parents picked up whatever was handy. When Robert was five, his mother struck him so hard in the back of the head with a piece of firewood that the boy fell unconscious on the kitchen floor and had to be revived by his sister Florence, who poured cold water on him. On another occasion Margaret Garrow split young Robert's head open with a crowbar.

The Garrow children's sex education came early in the form of all of them sleeping in the house's one bedroom with their parents. Each night the youngsters listened to their parents making love. Yet if Robert or the other children so much as brought up the subject of sex in their house, they were severely beaten.

When he turned seven, Robert was boarded out to the Maholleck farm in nearby Moriah, where he lived and worked for the next eight years. He was allowed to come home on Saturday night, when his father was paid for the boy's week of toil on the farm. Though the Mahollecks' were fair and loving people who treated Robert well, the boy had no playmates. He longed to return home, no matter that it was unhappy and brutal, so he might have the companionship of his sisters and brother.

In what was to become his frequent and only form of youthful sexual gratification, Robert began having sex with the animals on the Maholleck farm during his eleventh year. He had intercourse with dogs, cows, horses, and sheep. Also about that time, Robert fell into the macabre practice of drinking the blood of animals he slaughtered as part of his farm chores.

Robert got into some trouble when he was fifteen. One Saturday night he hot-wired one of the Mahollecks' trucks and drove to Port Henry with a couple of guys he knew, looking for girls. The truck's engine blew up on the way back to Moriah and, as punishment for stealing the truck, Robert was fired from his job and sent home. When he arrived at his house, the boy was set upon by his drunken father for being discharged by the Mahollecks. By this time Robert had developed into a powerful young man, and he split his father's face open with a single punch. The following day his parents visited the courthouse and convinced the local judge to issue a writ of incorrigibility on their son. Young Robert was sent under court order to live at the State Industrial School near Rochester, where he remained until he turned seventeen, at which time he enlisted in the Air Force.

Robert Garrow's military career lasted only two years. His service problems began in basic training, where he was severely ridiculed by his fellow enlisted men and his officers for wetting the bed. After completing basic training, Garrow was sent to Florida. While stationed there, an incident occurred in which he confiscated his sergeant's camera to even a debt. As a consequence he was sentenced to six months in the military prison at Eglan Air Force Base in Florida, from which he promptly escaped. Once apprehended, he received an additional one-year sentence for escaping and was sent to the stockade at Camp Gordon, Georgia. He served out his sentence and, upon release, was granted a medical discharge due to his incontinence and his demonstrated inability to adjust to military life. Of his two years in military service, Garrow had spent all but a few months in the stockade.

Garrow migrated north. After working a short time for Railway Express in Albany, New York, he found his way back to northern New York. He hired out on a farm near Lowville, in the Adirondacks, where he met Edith at a dance. They were married in Albany on June 23, 1957.

Once he and his wife moved to Albany, Garrow began having trouble with the law. He was charged with burglarizing the fast-food restaurant in which he had formerly worked—he claimed his ex-employer owed him back pay and that he was only trying to get what was rightfully his. In 1961 Garrow was arrested for raping a young woman and beating her boyfriend unconscious. He was convicted and served eight years in Dannemora and Auburn state prisons.

To close the circle on Robert Garrow's personality profile, Frank Armani interviewed Dr. Walter Osinski, director of Albany County Mental Health, and the court-appointed psychiatrist who had examined Garrow in 1961 before his trial for the rape and assault charges. Osinski told Armani that he had found Garrow to be an incipient psychotic, a mental disturbance that didn't fit into any particular neurotic or psychotic pattern. Osinski had recommended in 1961 that Garrow receive psychiatric treatment, but the psychiatrist's recommendation was never acted upon. Garrow received no treatment during his eight years in Dannemora and Auburn.

In response to Armani's questions, the psychiatrist would not come out and state that the Domblewski murder was an absolute indicator that Garrow was suffering from a mental disease. Osinski believed Garrow's sexual aberrations and violent rages were interrelated; so that Garrow would accost a couple, get angry at the man, then rape the woman. Dr. Osinski also asserted that there was a high probability that the head injury suffered in the 1972 automobile accident was the basis for Garrow's violent headaches.

9

End of August · 1973

Exhausted, Armani negotiated his Mercedes along the on-ramp on Route 81 in Syracuse. Over the past couple of weeks he had spent more time behind the steering wheel of his car than he had at home. Running all over the state to interview Garrow family members and psychiatrists was wearing him out. Even more exhausting and time-consuming was commuting to Champlain Valley Physicians Hospital in Plattsburgh several times a week to speak with Garrow.

The murder suspect was proving to be a king-sized pain in the neck. He was on the phone to Armani practically every day claiming that he had more to reveal about his case and requesting that his lawyer come to Plattsburgh. Inevitably, all Armani got from his client in return for the five-hour drive to the hospital was a verbal runaround. Garrow, it seemed, wanted companionship more than he wanted to confide in his attorney.

Driving north on Interstate 81, Armani was sorting through some of the loose ends in the Garrow case. There was so much left to do. There were so many unanswered questions about the suspect's behavior and whereabouts in the weeks prior to the Domblewski murder, questions that needed answering before Armani could piece together his defense. Of one thing, though, the lawyer was certain: Garrow was insane, and rather than being sent to prison, he needed placement in a mental institution.

The law was specific about the fate of someone judged innocent of murder by reason of insanity—that person was committed to a state mental institution until he or she was determined by a panel of psychiatrists to be sane enough to return to society. Based on what Armani had learned from Dr. Walter Osinski and from the other psychiatrists he had consulted with, he felt certain that Garrow would never get any better, that his mental condition would only worsen with time, so that he would never be allowed to go free. This, in addition to the insanity plea being the correct defense tactic under the circumstances, was important to Armani. As the father of two teenaged daughters, he could never rest easy knowing that someone like Garrow was walking the streets.

On the other hand, Armani's obligation was to provide his client the best counsel possible, even if that meant Garrow might be found innocent by a jury of his peers of murdering Philip Domblewski. In this sense Armani was laboring under the classic paradox faced by every attorney who defends someone in a court of law: Getting to the truth is *not* the defense lawyer's paramount aim. That is the duty of the prosecution. The defense attorney is there in part to preserve the dignity of the individual and otherwise to ensure that the state doesn't deprive a client of life, liberty, or property without due process. To that end, the Constitution, along with the bar association's code of ethics, required Armani to do everything possible to ensure that Robert Garrow's dignity and rights were maintained during the trial, regardless of whether or not the will of the state and the prosecutor's search for the truth were frustrated. If he skillfully did his job and in so doing helped frustrate the prosecutor's search for the truth, Armani could be instrumental in Robert Garrow becoming a free man once again. To Armani, that was an extremely perturbing possibility.

Still another aspect of this case bothered Armani. It was taking up most of his time; his other work was sliding. As it became apparent that he couldn't devote his energy to some of his other clients, and as some of them began complaining because their legal needs weren't being met, Armani had had to turn many of his files over to the other three lawyers in his office. Armani felt a certain amount of guilt over not personally attending to his other clients' needs and for spending so much time and effort on a case that wouldn't pay much. His law partners shared in the firm's profits, profits certain to be decreased by the Garrow case. Although they didn't openly complain, they would've preferred that Armani utilize his time going after corporate accounts or suing malpractice and insurance cases. Those were the big money cases. Murder trials, unless you were defending a wealthy client, didn't even pay the light bill.

So it was with a sense of guilt that Armani moved ahead with constructing Robert Garrow's defense. However, the mechanics of assembling the reams of material and evidence necessary to prepare for a trial of this magnitude, though physically and mentally debilitating, fascinated him. Interviewing witnesses and plowing through legal and psychiatric texts were Armani's forte; he loved doing the backup research.

The prospect of conducting Garrow's defense in the courtroom was another matter. That key aspect of the case, though the trial probably wouldn't get under way for another nine months, had been causing Armani a great deal of trepidation. That was the reason he was taking the long way to Plattsburgh on this muggy, cloudy Sunday afternoon. Armani planned to stop by Francis Belge's summer home in Henderson Harbor.

When he reached the dirt-and-grass driveway leading to Belges' home, which fronted on Lake Ontario, Armani realized that he hadn't seen his friend since that morning in the delicatessen when Belge had sharply criticized him for appearing on television to ask his client to give himself up.

Francis Belge was sitting in a wooden lawn chair in the front yard of his summer home. He wore shorts and no shirt, was deeply tanned, and appeared fit. Binoculars to his face, Belge was watching sailboats lean into the harbor's stiff westerly wind. Dressed in a suit and tie, Armani ambled across the plush, neatly trimmed lawn and came to a halt behind Belge.

"How are you, Frank?" Belge asked without taking the field glasses from his eyes.

"About three steps from a nervous breakdown, but otherwise okay."

"Drink?" Belge asked. He lowered the binoculars and pulled a shaker full of martinis out from under the lawn chair.

"Pass," Armani answered.

"This Garrow case is kicking my butt, Belge."

"Don't say I didn't tell you so."

"The thing keeps getting bigger and more involved every day."

"You mean about the cops figuring Garrow also grabbed off the Hauck girl?"

Alicia Hauck, a sixteen-year-old high school student, had been missing since July. She had disappeared on her way home from summer session at Corcoran High School. Robert Garrow had been placed in the area the day she had disappeared and was a prime suspect in the case.

"Not only the Hauck girl," Armani explained. "They are also building cases against Garrow for the Porter murder and Petz abduction. I could be in court for five years with this guy."

"What do you want from me, Frank?" Belge brought the field glasses back up to his face.

"I need someone I can depend on; I need help with Garrow. He won't tell me a thing."

"Of course he won't. The guy knows that he's going to swing. Your only hope to get him to cooperate with you is to sell him on the idea that you can make a deal with the DA—Garrow's confession for a lifetime pass to a mental institution."

Armani thought about that one. Plea bargain a killer? One of the most hated and feared men in New York State history? It'd be a tough sell.

"Like I said to you before," Armani remarked, "I got the feeling that this case is going to be famous. It can make us—"

"Make us nuts."

Armani decided on another approach. "Will you at least come to the hospital this afternoon with me and help me get something out of Garrow?"

A reflective Belge stared out at the boats making the turn at the marker buoy. Armani nervously played with the laces of his black, wing-tip shoes.

"All right, I'll ride up there with you," Belge said finally. "But no deal on my acting as your co-counsel on this kamikaze case. I'd just like to meet this maniac you're defending."

Armani's craggy face split into a smile. At least he had his foot in the door with Belge.

Belge changed into slacks and a sport shirt and climbed into the passenger seat of his friend's Mercedes. Armani took Route 69 eastward, then cut over Route 8 toward Speculator. Along the way, at Belge's suggestion, they stopped at a couple of country inns. Belge had done a lot of deer hunting in the area and knew many of the innkeepers. He wanted to get a feel from the Adirondack locals about Garrow's chances of receiving a fair trial in Hamilton County. In talking to people they met in the bars, Armani's worst fears were borne out. Without exception, these locals felt that Garrow was guilty. Many believed the county should spare itself the expense of the trial by allowing the murder suspect to escape into the muzzles of some well-chosen, anonymously fired rifles.

At one of the inns, Belge and Armani ran into a friend of Henry LaBlanc, the conservation officer who had shot Garrow in Witherbee. The fellow claimed that LaBlanc was a dead shot, except for his habit of closing his eyes when he pulled the trigger. If LaBlanc had kept his eyes open, the man said laughingly, everyone would have been spared a lot of trouble and money.

The two lawyers arrived at Champlain Valley Physicians Hospital late that afternoon. They made their way through the heavily guarded lobby, up the elevator, to the fifth floor. Armani led Belge past the two troopers sealing off the hallway leading to Garrow's room. Outside the suspect's door sat another trooper.

"I'm here to see my client," Armani announced.

The trooper nodded, then fixed his eyes on Belge.

"This is Francis Belge, my co-counsel on this case." Armani identified Belge as such in order to get him past the guard.

Belge began to follow Armani into Garrow's room.

"Hold it," the trooper ordered. He jumped to his feet and grabbed Belge's right arm. The trooper stood at least six inches taller than Belge and was built like a refrigerator with arms. "You're the only one allowed in there, Armani."

"I told you he's my co-counsel. . . ." Armani's words trailed off when Belge yanked away from the trooper's grip.

"Take your hands off me!" Belge hissed.

"And I said you ain't going into that room," the trooper challenged, grabbing the front of Belge's shirt.

What happened next occurred so fast that Armani had no chance to get between the two men. Belge, in an attempt to free himself from the trooper's grip, shoved the uniformed man so hard his hat flipped off. The trooper retaliated by pushing the lawyer halfway across the hall, ripping the buttons from Belge's shirt as he did.

"Who the hell do you think you are?" Belge shouted and shoved back at the strapping trooper.

Armani stood dumbfounded while Belge and the trooper grabbed and cursed at one another. The lawyer appeared to be getting the best of the cop when two other troopers rushed down the hall and jammed Belge roughly against the wall.

Belge's face was red with fury. He called over the troopers' shoulders to his friend, "All right, Armani, you've got yourself a co-counsel. These jerks are going to find out that when they mess with a bull they get the horns."

"Let him go, willya," Armani said, trying to wedge himself between the burly troopers and Belge. "He's an officer of the court, fer cryin' out loud."

"I don't give a rat's ass if this clown is the governor," the hatless trooper with the crew cut stated. "Unless we get orders, nobody but you goes into that room."

"Okay. Okay. I'll call Henry McCabe and get clearance," a winded Armani answered. He hustled down the hall to the pay phone. He turned around after the dime dropped into the slot. Belge was grinning wickedly into the dour, sweating faces of the troopers who had him pinned against the wall.

It wasn't easy to get Belge cleared to enter Garrow's room. Armani had to make several calls to track McCabe down. He finally located the BCI investigator at the state police lab in Albany, only to be advised that McCabe didn't have the authority to allow Belge into Garrow's hospital room. That permission would have to come from District Judge George Marthen. It took another three calls before Armani was able to speak with Marthen. The judge was acquainted with Francis Belge by reputation and quickly assented to Armani's request to use Belge as co-counsel on the Garrow case. Marthen volunteered to call Henry McCabe at the police lab in Albany and issue clearance for Belge to enter the suspect's room. Armani asked Marthen to have McCabe call right back so the BCI investigator could advise his men to allow Belge into Garrow's room.

Less than ten minutes later Armani introduced Francis Belge to Robert Garrow and carefully advised the murder suspect of his new co-counsel's credentials as a trial lawyer.

Garrow was initially put off by the idea that Armani had enlisted Belge's aid on his case. The suspect was highly suspicious of anyone but Armani, an attitude that caused the evening's session to be unproductive. He led the two attorneys around in circles, claiming lapses of memory for the periods during June and July for which he had no alibi. Belge had to pry from Garrow information that the suspect had already revealed to Armani. Once again Garrow fell into his old routine of complaining about rough treatment from the contingent of troopers guarding him. Further, he seemed angered by Belge's manner of asking questions, which was more direct and less conciliatory than Armani's. Where Armani chose to accept Garrow's allegations that he couldn't remember what had occurred at certain times, Belge, in an attempt to get at the truth, continually confronted the suspect about some of his statements. Belge's impatience and occasional abrasiveness also bothered Armani. He was afraid of losing whatever confidence he had built up with Garrow over the past weeks.

After four hours of getting nowhere, Armani and Belge called it quits. They advised Garrow that they would be staying the night in a local motel and would come back the following morning to continue the questioning.

10

The Following Morning

FRANK ARMANI had learned hypnosis several years earlier. It
was a skill that he used mostly at parties, to entertain friends by
putting someone under and have the hypnotized person perform small harmless tricks. He used hypnosis only sparingly in
his professional life. Armani knew that information obtained
from someone under hypnosis could be ruled inadmissable as
evidence in a court of law. The technique was too unreliable
and the hypnotized person too prone to the power of suggestion.

But so frustrated was he in his attempts to get past Garrow's
memory block about certain critical periods during the previous June and July that the lawyer decided to hypnotize his client. He would do it alone with Garrow, while Belge spent the
morning in the motel listening to tapes of previous interviews
Armani had conducted with Garrow and his family.

When Armani entered Garrow's room, the murder suspect
was seated in the chair next to his bed. His shattered left leg
held straight out by a cast that ran from his toes to his hip,
Garrow was busily reading newspaper clippings of the manhunt and his subsequent capture. Though his face was still pale
and gaunt, Garrow's eyes were clear behind his black-rimmed
glasses.

"Morning, Frank," Garrow greeted him.

"Did you sleep okay?"

"Yeah, good," Garrow answered. His mouth seemed to have lost the exaggerated movement painkillers induce. He watched Armani set his tape recorder on the nightstand. "Look, Frank, I'm sorry if I acted funny last night when you introduced me to that guy, Belge. I just wish you would have checked with me before bringing him in on my case."

"What you're going to have to understand, Bob," Armani stated firmly, "is that if I'm going to be of any help to you, you're going to have to trust me. I wouldn't have asked Belge to come in on this thing with me unless I was certain he could do us some good. I *need* him on your case."

"If you say so, Frank, it's good enough for me."

"You're going to have to trust me about everything, if you expect me to do you any good," Armani continued, adjusting his chair so he faced his client. He glanced at Garrow's wounded left arm. The healing skin was pink and sagging, the arm rail-thin—the signs of atrophy. "If you want even a prayer of beating this thing, I'm going to have to know *everything*. You can't hold anything back from me."

"I've told you all I can remember, Frank. Just keep askin' me things, willya, and I'll see if I can give you something that'll help you."

"We've done enough of that," Armani retorted, watching Garrow's eyes closely. He had learned in past sessions that if he pushed Garrow too far and too fast, the suspect's eyes would narrow in anger and then he would clam up. "We're not covering enough ground. I'm running out of time."

Garrow nodded.

"Like I've said to you before, they've got you cold on the Domblewski murder. Three witnesses have placed you with the kid at the moment he was stabbed to death. They got your knife, the one you bought at Sears. Your fingerprints are all over it, as is Domblewski's blood."

Garrow stared sullenly at Armani.

"They're also building a case against you on the Porter murder and on the Petz disappearance. Plus they're trying to tie you to the disappearance of Alicia Hauck in Syracuse. Now, I've showed you pictures of those three kids, and you said you don't know them. Is that right?"

"I swear to you, Frank, I don't know anything about those other kids."

"I believe you, Bob," Armani said, choosing his words carefully. "I believe that you don't know anything about Porter, Petz, and Hauck. But there are so many details about certain periods of time during the summer that you *can't* remember, I need to be certain that you don't have any information hidden deep in your subconscious, vital information that the cops might know that will hurt us when you go to trial. Do you understand what I'm saying?"

"I think so. You want to see if I'm forgetting something that might help you defend me."

"That's it. Something buried deep in your mind that you can't recall. Now, there is one method that will help us get beyond that block in your mind that prevents you from remembering certain occurrences. Are you familiar with hypnosis, Bob?"

"Just what I've read about it."

"It's a perfectly harmless technique that'll make it easier for you to recall what happened during those times in June and July that are blanks for you. Would you be willing let me try to hypnotize you?"

"Yeah, that would be okay. If it would give you anything that would help you," Garrow answered. He appeared confident, as though he had nothing to hide.

"Okay," Armani said, lighting a cigarette. "I want you to get comfortable. As comfortable as you can get in that cast."

Garrow shifted in his chair.

"You think you'd be more relaxed if you were in bed?"

"Naw, Frank, this is okay."

Armani checked that his tape recorder was functioning properly, then turned to face his client. He held his smoldering cigarette in front of Garrow's face and began. "All right now, Bob, I want you to stare at the ember on the end of this cigarette. Real close. Try not to blink. . . . That's it. . . . That's it. . . ."

Holding the cigarette very still, Armani continued in an even, soft voice, "You're going to feel your eyes watering. . . . Now start blinking. . . . Go ahead, Bob, blink . . . because you feel as though there are small magnets on the upper and lower lids of your right eye, and on the upper and lower lids of your left eye. The lids of your right eye are wanting to come together. The magnets want to meet. . . . The lids of your left eye are also wanting to come together. . . . The magnets in your left eye want to meet. . . . Your lids want to come together . . . and stay together. . . ."

Garrow's eyes blinked in an exaggerated fashion a couple of times, then drooped slowly shut.

"Okay now Bob, I want you to picture yourself as being in the most relaxed place that you can imagine. Maybe lying in lush grass next to a mountain stream on a nice sunny summer day. You're relaxed, totally relaxed. . . . You feel yourself drifting . . . drifting . . . drifting," Armani continued in a soothing, deep voice.

After a few more minutes of talking gently to Garrow, Armani had him imagine that there was a helium balloon attached to his good wrist. He convinced Garrow that the imaginary balloon was slowly going to lift his arm. Once Garrow had raised his arm to eye level, the lawyer instructed him that the balloon was losing its lift, so that his arm would lower slowly. When Garrow's arm was back on his thigh, Armani was convinced by his responsiveness and level of relaxation that he was in a hypnotic state.

"Okay, Bob, I want you to keep that picture in your mind of you resting next to that mountain stream. See yourself resting comfortably. I'm going to wake you soon. And when I do, I want you to know in your mind that you will be free to answer any questions that Mr. Belge asks you about those times in June and July that were previously a blank to you. You will be able to answer any questions he asks you. . . ."

Armani paused to let that suggestion take hold.

"All right, Bob, I want you to slowly open your eyes . . . nice and slow. That's it. You're waking up. . . . That's right."

Garrow's eyelids parted, and he gazed at Armani with the trusting gentleness of someone waking from a refreshing sleep.

That afternoon it was Francis Belge's turn to be alone with Garrow. The two lawyers had agreed that Garrow would be less distracted in responding to Armani's hypnotic suggestion if Belge handled the afternoon session by himself.

The first thing Belge did when he walked into Garrow's room was turn on the television and portable room fan. The attorney understood well the lengths to which the BCI would go to make this case. Belge felt certain that Garrow's room was bugged and counted on the TV and fan noise to camouflage his interview with Garrow.

"Okay, Bob," Belge began in his matter-of-fact, confidently brusque manner. "Frank Armani has told you that I'm one of the best criminal lawyers in New York State."

"He did," Garrow answered. Again seated in the chair next to his bed and sipping a cup of coffee, Garrow watched Belge set up the portable tape recorder. The attorney arranged the mike so it was close to Garrow's face.

"So you understand that I know what I'm doing," Belge continued, sliding a chair in front of Garrow.

"If Frank says to trust you, I do."

Belge noticed right off that Garrow seemed different from the previous night, when the attorney had last spoken with him. Garrow's eyes appeared sharper and more focused, his face more intent. His responses were quick and to the point, and the whining tone was absent from his voice.

"Okay. First I want you to talk directly into this mike," Belge instructed, sliding the mike stand closer to Garrow's face. "That way the recorder will pick you up over the fan and TV."

Garrow leaned forward so his lips were only inches from the mike.

"Now, listen carefully to me, Bob," Belge continued, moving his face closer to Garrow's. "Your *only* chance in that courtroom will be a plea of innocent by reason of insanity. You know that, I know that, Frank Armani knows that, and the prosecution knows that. I want you to realize that an insanity plea is very hard to prove in a court of law. For every shrink I can produce who says you're nuts and can't be held responsible for your crime, the prosecution can produce another one to swear that you're sane. Psychiatry and psychology aren't exact sciences."

Belge watched Garrow as the information sank in. Garrow sat mute, his eyes alert and jaw muscles jumping.

"Our best shot is to make a deal beforehand—cop a plea with the DA before your case goes to trial, so that you'll be sent to a hospital rather than to prison. You'd like that, wouldn't you, Bob? A hospital rather than prison?"

Garrow nodded. "I'll never stay alive in prison. I'd prefer to get shot down like a dog trying to escape from this hospital than go to the penitentiary."

"I don't blame you," Belge agreed. "But in order to cop a

plea with the DA, I'm going to need something to bargain with. We got no room to maneuver on the Domblewski killing. They have you on that one. I'm going to need to give the DA something from you that they don't already have, some crucial information that they want badly but haven't been able to get on their own. You understand what I'm referring to, don't you, Bob?"

Belge paused so that Garrow could consider fully what he had said.

"Now I want to ask you about Alicia Hauck. The girl who disappeared July eleventh on her way home from Corcoran High School. According to Frank Armani's records, you missed work that day. The Syracuse cops have placed you in the area of Corcoran High School on July eleventh. Now, I want you to fill me in on what happened that day."

Garrow removed his glasses and rubbed a hand nervously across his forehead. He was sweating. His face was flushed. His eyes had dulled and seemed turned inward.

"C'mon, Bob. If you want me to make a deal for you, you have to help me," Belge prodded, leaning forward until his face was only inches from Garrow's. The lawyer's tone was gentle and friendly, yet probing. "If I've got some more killings to talk with the DA about, it'll show that you're insane—that you didn't just murder Domblewski out of anger or whatever."

"I picked her up hitchhiking," Garrow admitted.

"Talk into the mike," Belge reminded, trying to keep his enthusiasm in check. "Otherwise the machine won't pick you up over the noise."

Garrow turned toward the mike and, with more emphasis, repeated, "I picked her up hitchhiking."

"You mean the Hauck girl?"

"Yeah, that's her. I learned her name from reading the Syracuse papers the next day."

"So what happened after you picked her up hitchhiking?"

"We drove up to some apartments near my house. You know the ones? On the hill, near Syracuse University?"

"The Vincent Apartments?" Belge filled in. He noted the transformation in Garrow's manner. The man's voice was lower and more certain and his tone cold and calculating.

"Yeah, those are the ones," Garrow clarified.

"What happened up there?"

"We had sex on the hill behind the apartments."

"Did she resist?"

"Yeah," Garrow answered quietly.

"Then what happened?"

"I made her walk with me into Oakwood Cemetery. We had been walking and talking for some time when, all of a sudden and for no reason, she tried to run away. When I tried to talk her into staying with me for a little while more, she got hysterical. I got scared and hit her with my knife."

"You mean you stabbed her?" an astonished Belge asked.

"Yeah, I hit her with my knife."

"Did you kill her?"

"I think so."

"You *think* so?"

"Yeah, she was dead," Garrow explained, avoiding Belge's eyes.

"What did you do with her body?"

"I stashed it in a deserted corner of the cemetery. In the underbrush behind the maintenance shack."

"Okay, Bob," Belge cut in. "You can tell me exactly where you hid Alicia Hauck's body later. I want to hear about the Petz girl. The girl who disappeared near Wevertown. The police think you had something to do with her disappearance."

Once again Garrow wiped the sweat from his forehead with his good hand. "I was on the way to visit my parents, and I pulled off the road."

"Near Wevertown?"

"Yeah, that's it. On a small country road. I wanted to get some sleep. A short time later I was awakened by a car horn. First thing I noticed was that I had an awful headache. Anyway, the driver of the other car, a hippy kid, walked up to my car. I was still sitting in the front seat, and this guy started yelling at me to move my car."

"Was it Daniel Porter who yelled at you to move your car?"

"I don't know who he was. That's the name the cops used, though."

"So what happened when he yelled at you?"

"I got out of my car. That's when I saw the girl."

"Susan Petz?"

"I don't know her name. I thought it was Carol."

"Tell me what happened when you got out of your car?"

"I was standing on the road, and this guy started shoving me and stuff. When I grabbed him back, the girl hit me in the head. *Kapow!* Just like that," Garrow said and rolled his head as though he had just been struck. "Anyway, the guy and I started fighting. When we fell into the ditch alongside the road, he got stabbed."

"Got stabbed when you rolled into the ditch? Bob, when they found Porter, he was tied to a tree."

"I don't remember anything about that. Honest," Garrow insisted. "The only thing I know was that when we were in the ditch, I hit him with my knife."

"Did you kill him?"

"I think he was dead, yeah."

"So what did you do with the girl?"

"I took her with me. We drove in my car to Mineville, where my parents live. My father had just had a heart attack, and I was bringing him a cane I bought for him in Syracuse."

The paradox of Garrow acting the role of a dutiful son by driving four hours to bring his father a cane and on the way killing one person and kidnapping another stunned Belge. "What did you do with the Petz girl once you reached Mineville?"

"I pitched my tent up on Barton Hill, up above my parents' house. You familiar with the area?"

"Not really."

"Big hill, heavily wooded, up above the old Republic Steel Mine. I kept the girl up there in the tent with me."

"How long did you have her?"

"Three days."

"Did you have sex with her?"

"Yeah."

"Did the Petz girl try to fight you off?"

"Yeah, she tried to fight me off," Garrow admitted, using the same dejected tone he had employed when he disclosed that Alicia Hauck had also resisted him. It was as though admitting that he'd had to resort to rape somehow took away from his manhood and attractiveness to women.

Belge, feeling an inner revulsion about all of this, paused.

"Plus, we talked," Garrow picked up, as if trying to redeem himself. "We had great conversations, her and I. She told me about the college she went to. Stuff like that."

"You said you kept her in the tent with you for three days. Did you stay with her all that time?" Belge asked.

"Naw. I visited my parents and my sister Agnes. She lives in Witherbee, right across the gorge from Mineville."

"Did you sleep in the tent at night with the Petz girl?"

"I stayed at my sister Agnes's."

"How did you prevent the Petz girl from escaping while you were gone from the tent?"

"I tied her up at night with hose clamps and ropes. I left her food and water."

"You mean she couldn't have untied herself and walked out of the woods?"

"She didn't know where she was. It's real desolate up on Barton Hill. For all she knew, she could've been a hundred miles from anywhere."

"What happened to her?"

"On the afternoon of the fourth day we were together, it was hotter than hell and I wanted to go swimming. I made her go down the hill with me. There's a spring down there that Republic Steel used before they closed down the mine. I put my knife on the ground, and she grabbed it. We had a fight. She cut my hand. I finally got my knife away from her, and she got stabbed."

"You mean you killed her?"

"She was dead."

"What did you do with her body?"

"I shoved it down the airshaft of the mine."

Belge leaned forward, and spoke directly into Garrow's face. "The cops have been all over that area. How come they haven't found the Petz girl's body?"

"I hid it good. Put it way down in the airshaft and covered it with old tires and timbers from the mine."

"What did you do about your cut hand? Didn't anyone ask how you got hurt?"

"I went over to Agnes's house. I told her I'd cut it when I fell while camping. She fixed it up for me."

A confused, shaken Francis Belge sat back in the chair. Part of him doubted what Garrow had just told him. He wanted to believe that Garrow was deranged enough to create a story just to convince his lawyers that he was insane, so they would make a deal with the authorities on his behalf. But something in Garrow's manner—the suspect's calculating, businesslike attitude—convinced him that he was telling the truth. Further, Belge figured that Garrow wasn't so unbalanced that he'd fabricate a story that easy to check. If his lawyers couldn't locate the bodies, his confession would obviously be bogus.

"How about some of these other murders the cops have you figured for?"

"That's all I done. I swear."

"How about the map McCabe found in your car? The one with the dots and girls' names spotted all over the state?"

"I don't know anything about that map," Garrow answered, his eyes narrowing with anger. "I didn't have any map in my glove compartment. I figure that the BCI planted it."

"Never mind about that for now." Belge saw the fury building in Garrow, and he didn't want to chance losing his client's confidence and openness. "You're saying that you committed only four murders?"

"Just the four. I swear to you."

"You sure, Bob? Better to give me everything now, before I talk with the DA. If I make a deal with him and it comes out that you've left something out, you can be prosecuted for it later."

"That's it. I'm tellin' you." Garrow's face softened into a smile. "You need some more for the DA, I can give 'em to you. Be real easy around this place."

"No, please, no more. I've got enough." Belge laughed nervously. "Okay, tell me exactly where you stashed Alicia Hauck's body."

"If you walk directly west from the maintenance shack in Oakwood Cemetery, about a hundred paces, you'll find it in the bushes."

Belge reached over and snapped off the tape recorder. He rose wearily and stuffed the recorder into his briefcase.

"You sit tight. Frank and I will be back to you in a few days."

"You don't tell the cops anything about this, unless you talk with me first?"

"Whatever you've told me is privileged information, Bob. I'm bound by the law not to tell anyone—that is, unless you release me from this confidentiality. Until then, it's like you've told a priest in a confessional. My lips, as are Frank Armani's, are sealed about this."

Belge opened the door of Garrow's room. As he was leaving, he turned for one final look at his client. The murder suspect had a small, coy smile on his lips.

11

Later That Afternoon

I THINK THE BASTARD IS conning us," Armani said as he eased his Mercedes onto Interstate 87. He and Belge were on their way to Mineville, forty miles south of Plattsburgh. As they drove, they listened to the cassette recording of Garrow explaining how he had killed Alicia Hauck, Daniel Porter, and Susan Petz.

"You mean you *hope* he's conning us," Belge answered.

Belge was right. Armani *was* hoping that Garrow was simply a nut who had made up his story about killing the three young people just to induce his lawyers to make a deal for him. Armani gave some thought as to whether Garrow had invented or confabulated the story as a means of responding to the hypnotic suggestion to "answer every question Belge asks you."

"I think we have a problem," Belge said, ending Armani's silent speculations about the reliability of hypnosis. "If you'll check your rearview mirror, you'll note that there is a familiar gray car following us. It's been on our butt since we left the hospital."

As if afraid the driver of the car tailing them might see him do it, Armani shifted his eyes slowly to the rearview mirror. He recognized the Ford sedan as an unmarked BCI vehicle.

"So what do we do?" Armani asked.

"Just drive. It would make sense that we'd be going to

Mineville. Garrow's parents live there, and we need to have a talk with them."

The two lawyers continued driving south on Interstate 87. The tape of Belge's interview with Garrow played on, and Armani grew more sickened at what he was hearing.

Once off the interstate, they headed down a back road through hill country toward Mineville. It was then that Belge noticed a single-engine plane overhead.

"Looks like they've got their air force tailing us, too," Belge said.

The two men bent to see through the upper part of the windshield. The plane passed overhead, made a wide turn in front of them, and came back for a second look.

A short time later Belge and Armani reached Mineville, a hamlet of dusty frame buildings located in the crotch of stunted mountains. Several people stood at curbside in the mostly boarded-up business district, carefully watching Armani's expensive car roll past.

"This place should be in the Appalachians," Belge commented. "Tobacco Road revisited."

"Palm Springs it's not."

"Pull into that gin mill," Belge ordered, pointing at the small tavern on their right. "We'll have a couple of pops and make some calls."

Armani eased his Mercedes to a stop in the gravel lot. They left the cassette of Belge's interview with Garrow in the car's tapedeck and locked the doors. The dark bar they stepped into reeked of stale beer and greasy food. There were several men standing at the long bar, and all of them stared hard at the well-groomed, affluent-looking lawyers.

"A club soda for my friend and a very dry Tanqueray martini for me, on the rocks," Belge ordered as he and Armani stepped to a vacant spot at the bar.

The tall, emphysemic-looking bartender appeared confused. Belge saw it and added, "Just fill a glass with ice and gin and wave it toward Italy."

The gray-faced bartender blinked.

"House gin with a dash of vermouth," Belge clarified, rolling his eyes.

Once they had their drinks in hand, Armani and Belge turned their attention to one another.

"I'm going to call Garrow's parents and tell them we'll be up in a couple of hours," Belge explained.

"A couple of hours? We ain't gonna hang around this joint for a couple of hours?" Armani asked. The men at the bar were eyeing them as if they were from another planet, and it made Armani uncomfortable.

"Just trust me, Frank," Belge added. He pushed away from the bar.

While Belge walked to the back of the tavern to where the pay phone was located, Armani huddled over his drink. If he had thought to glance out the saloon's front window, he would have seen the gray car that had been following them ease to a stop across the street. Henry McCabe was in the passenger seat. He was talking to his driver, a crew-cut, sallow-faced agent about McCabe's age.

The driver stepped from the car and walked slowly over to Armani's Mercedes. He peered in the window, noted something, then returned to the gray car.

"The cassette is still in the deck," the man said, adjusting his wire-rimmed, reflector sunglasses.

"What do you suggest we do?" McCabe asked.

"Maybe we should handle it the way those two agents did in that tax fraud case they made. They hot-wired the car, drove it to Canada, confiscated the evidence, then burned the car," the agent offered with a smile.

"Don't think so," McCabe answered. "We'll just wait until they come out, then continue tailing them. I got the feeling that they'll show us what's on that tape."

Inside the bar, Belge had rejoined Armani. He took to staring at his drink as if challenging the martini to see who was going to get the best of whom on this day. Then in a swift motion, he grabbed the glass from the bar and knocked back the drink in one long swallow. He stood back, shook a bit, and, like a tree that miraculously blooms when struck by lightning, came to life.

"Okay, counselor, let's go." Belge slapped his hands together.

Armani paid the bar tab and followed Belge out of the tavern. Once in the car Belge directed Armani to head out of town, away from Mineville.

"Where the hell are we going?" Armani asked.

"To Tupper Lake. There's a broad going to meet us there."

"A broad?" Armani asked incredulously. "We've got work to do, Belge."

"You've got to have a little faith and trust in me, Frank," Belge answered, flashing a devilish smile. He turned his head slightly and noted the gray car about a half mile behind them.

"Faith and trust?" Armani asked. "What the hell's the difference between the two?"

"You've been to the circus and seen that guy who walks the tightrope pushing the wheelbarrow?"

"What's *that* have to do with the price of linguine?"

"Well, you know that the guy has done that trick a couple of thousand times. So you figure he'll make it across. That's faith. Trust is being willing to sit in that wheelbarrow while he pushes it across the high wire. So climb into the wheelbarrow for me, willya, Frank?"

"Why do I have the feeling that you're getting me to crawl into a barrel instead of a wheelbarrow?" Armani laughed. With Belge as co-counsel, this case had lost some of its tedium for him.

Belge directed them to a country inn overlooking Tupper Lake. They left the Mercedes on the street and walked into the bar, where an attractive blonde in her late twenties awaited them. Belge moved up to her and kissed her on the mouth.

"Donna, say hello to Frank Armani."

"Heard a lot about you." The woman took Armani's hand.

"Nice to meet you," Armani answered. The woman was a knockout. She had sparkling green eyes, a sensuous mouth, and full breasts. She was wearing a short white skirt, and her shapely legs were deeply tanned. The woman spoke with an accent, Scandinavian, Armani guessed.

Belge ordered a round of drinks and fell into conversation with Donna. By the way he and she touched one another tenderly on the shoulder and legs as they talked, Armani figured the two were very intimate. Armani smiled to himself. Belge had girlfriends spaced around New York State, and he had the seductive knack of making each one feel as if she were the only woman in his life.

Meanwhile, out in front of the restaurant, Henry McCabe leaned back against the front seat of the Ford sedan and rested his neck on the headrest. "Might as well relax," he said. "We could be here for a while."

After about half an hour, the other agent noted a blond woman climbing into the driver's seat of Frank Armani's Mercedes. She inserted the key into the ignition and started the engine.

"What the hell!" he blurted.

McCabe watched the woman drive away in Armani's car. "Those bastards," he muttered.

"Should we follow her?" his partner asked, pulling himself up straight in the seat.

"Not unless you want to find out where she lives," McCabe answered. "My guess is that Armani and Belge walked out the back door of that joint and took off in her car."

"What about the cassette tape?"

"You don't really think they left it in the car this time, do you?" McCabe shook his head. "Let's get back to Plattsburgh."

As the BCI car peeled rubber making a U-turn across the highway, some twenty miles away Armani was easing Donna's blue Pinto up a secluded forestry road on Barton Hill in Mineville. Satisfied he was far enough off the main road so the Pinto couldn't be spotted by any car that happened by, he cut the engine.

"Damn, it's hot," Armani said as he climbed out of the air-conditioned car. He tugged at his shirt collar and removed his tie, which he stuck in his back pocket. "Must be a hundred degrees."

Belge had his portable tape recorder to his ear. "According to Garrow's instructions, we have to find the main entrance to the old mine. He said it's located about a half mile due west from this road."

The two lawyers bent into the steep mountain grade. Armani, wearing leather-soled shoes, slipped and nearly fell several times on the loose rocks. They had walked about a hundred feet when they felt it: A cold draft of air dried the sweat on their foreheads, then chilled them. The current of frigid air running down the mountain had stunted the growth of brush and trees in its path.

"Where the hell do you think that cold air is coming from?" Armani asked.

"Not sure," Belge responded, pausing to look up the mountain. "Probably from deep underground. Damn, it's eerie."

The two lawyers resumed their trek up the mountainside. They had walked another hundred feet or so, staying in the five-foot-wide channel of frigid air, when they spotted the main entrance to the mine. Rusted train tracks ran into a cloud of condensation that hung in the mouth of the mineshaft. Beyond that was darkness. The only noise to be heard was the sound of cold air rushing from the bowels of the earth.

Armani walked up to the gaping hole, which was surrounded on all sides by overgrown weeds and bushes, and peered in. "She in there?" he asked.

"Garrow claimed that he stashed the body in the airshaft," Belge clarified quietly. "That should be somewhere over here."

They made their way to the left of the mine entrance, around a cluster of house-sized boulders. Hidden among the advancing underbrush was a hole about three feet in diameter. Armani leaned over the edge. He could see down only a short distance.

"He said he killed her up there." Belge pointed to a flat area of ground about fifty feet from where they stood. Out of the hillside adjacent to the plateau ran a rusty pipe from which gurgled a stream of clear water. The water gathered into a small holding pond; the overflow from the pond wound its way as a gentle brook down the mountain.

"Garrow said he kept Susan Petz up on the mountain in his tent," Belge added, nodding toward the dense forest higher up the mountain.

"You really think she's in this airshaft?" Armani asked in a near whisper.

"Only one way to find out," Belge said. "Take off your belt and loop it through mine. That way you can hang onto me when I lean down and shine my flashlight."

Armani did as he was told. Once he had hooked his belt through Belge's, the blond lawyer, with Armani holding him back from falling, leaned over the edge and directed his flashlight into the airshaft.

"You see anything?" Armani asked in between grunting from supporting Belge's 190 pounds.

"Just some old tires and timbers . . . Hold it a minute!" an excited Belge exclaimed. "I think I see a tennis shoe."

Belge stared into the airshaft a few more seconds, then ordered, "Pull me up, Frank."

Armani did so. Once the two lawyers had regained their footing, they stood facing one another at the edge of the airshaft. Belge's complexion was gray, and he had tears in his eyes. He was unable to get any words out.

"Did you see her?" Armani asked.

"I think so . . . I mean, yeah."

Armani opened his Polaroid camera. "You hold me, and I'll get some pictures."

Armani threaded his belt through the loops of his pants. A still-shaken Belge secured his belt through Armani's, and lowered the shorter man into the mouth of the airshaft.

Even with the aid of the flashlight, Armani had to squint to see the pile of timbers and tires that rested on the ledge about ten feet below him. Protruding from the debris was a blue tennis shoe and the lower section of a small, lean left leg—Susan Petz's leg, Armani assumed. The leg was covered with frost. It had been perfectly preserved by the cold air.

"Oh, God. Oh, my God," Armani whispered. As he raised his camera, he felt sick to his stomach, and his entire body was coated with gooseflesh. He pressed the button, and the flash illuminated the upper portion of the airshaft. He stuffed the developing photo into the front of his open shirt, then snapped off another picture.

"All right," Armani called. "Get me out of here."

Belge pulled Armani out of the airshaft. Neither wanted to believe what he had seen. They stood alongside one another for a few minutes and stared into the dark hole.

"The rotten creep actually did it," Armani muttered angrily. "He killed that poor girl."

Belge nodded.

"So what now?"

"We get back to Syracuse and see if we can find Alicia Hauck's body."

"I mean we have to tell someone about what we've found. That girl's parents have to know."

"Unless Garrow gives us permission to do so, we can't say a word to anyone about what we've seen. You know that, Frank."

Armani only barely heard what Belge said. He was thinking

about how he would feel if that were his daughter down there? As a parent, wouldn't he want to know? But he also understood that Belge was correct. They were sworn to secrecy. The law prevented them from violating the sacred trust of privileged information that existed between them and Robert Garrow. For really the first time since he had been involved with the case, Frank Armani wished that he had never heard of Robert Garrow.

"Let's get out of here," Belge said and took a couple of steps away from the airshaft. He glanced back and saw Armani still staring into the dark hole.

"C'mon, Frank." Belge reached out and took Armani by the arm. "There's nothing we can do for that girl, now."

Saddened and disgusted, Armani followed Belge back down the mountain and out of reach of that evil blast of cold air that seemed to taint everything it touched.

12

The Following Day

EARLY THE NEXT MORNING, the two lawyers searched the
ground west of Oakwood Cemetery's maintenance building
where Garrow had indicated to Belge that he had left Alicia
Hauck's body. Though situated almost in the shadow of downtown Syracuse's high-rise buildings and at the border of the
Syracuse University campus, the sprawling cemetery was, in
the area of the maintenance building, as untamed as most wilderness areas. The tangle of trees, bushes, and undergrowth
through which the two lawyers tramped was nearly impenetrable.

Unable to locate the girl's remains, Belge and Armani returned to Plattsburgh to have Garrow draw them a map showing exactly where he had left Alicia Hauck. Once they had the
map, the two lawyers drove directly back to Syracuse and resumed the task of finding the girl's remains. By the time they
had stepped off the distance west of the maintenance building
to the patch of ground Garrow had instructed them to search,
dusk was rapidly dissolving into darkness. They were exhausted
and mosquito-bitten, their clothes were torn from fighting
through tenacious bramble bushes, and Armani had slipped
once and ripped open the knee of his suit pants.

Armani held his arm in front of him so his glasses wouldn't
be knocked from his face by the branches. "You sure we're in
the right spot?"

Belge rechecked Garrow's map. "She should be right around here someplace."

"Well, she isn't," Armani answered.

Belge paused and looked around. Even in full daylight, the rank growth would have kept visibility to less than three feet. Now that it was getting dark, it was worse. They would virtually have to trip over the girl's body to find it.

"Let's call it a day and come back tomorrow," Belge said.

"Why is it so blasted important that we *see* the body, anyway?" Armani asked. "Based on what we know about Garrow, we can safely assume that he killed the Hauck girl. Besides, aren't we taking a hell of a risk of someone spotting us tramping around here? We'll have a lot of explaining to do if the cops get onto this."

"Listen to him, willya?" Belge laughed. "We can't even find a body that's probably not more than five feet in front of us. How the hell is anyone going to see us?"

"Whatever." Armani began fighting his way back out of the underbrush. "I'm satisfied that he killed the Hauck girl. I see no reason to view her remains."

They made their way out of the cemetery and walked several blocks to where they had left Armani's Mercedes, which they had parked well outside the cemetery in order to throw off anyone who might be tailing them.

The following day, Belge returned to Oakwood Cemetery without Armani's knowledge. To help him locate Alicia Hauck's body, the attorney brought along an old friend and hunting guide, Ralph Kackison. Belge knew that if the girl's body was in the cemetery, Kackison could find it.

Kackison squared off the area of underbrush in which Garrow had indicated that he had left the body. He and Belge then walked every square of ground, eliminating areas as they searched them. After about an hour of wading through the underbrush, Kackison called to Belge. He had found the girl's remains.

Alicia Hauck's still partly clad body was badly decomposed and had been ravaged by animals. Her skull had been torn from her body, and was located ten feet from the rest of her remains. In an act that was later to cause him serious difficulties, Belge removed his handkerchief from his pocket and picked up the skull. He placed it above the girl's shoulders, then photographed the remains.

Upon leaving the cemetery, Belge explained to Kackison that they were bound by law not to reveal to anyone what they had just viewed. As far as anyone else was concerned, they had not found Alicia Hauck's body.

13

September 1973

It was just after eight o'clock at night. Armani sat in his deserted office. His heart was heavy with sadness as he studied the photograph Belge had taken of Alicia Hauck's animal-ravaged, decomposed remains. On his desk, next to the Polaroid photo, was a missing persons bulletin advertising the thousand-dollar reward Alicia's parents were offering for any information about their daughter. The picture on the missing persons bulletin had been taken when Alicia graduated from junior high school. She was wearing a white cap and gown and had long black hair, an oval pretty face, and dark eyes. She was listed as five feet tall and weighing 103 pounds.

He reached into one of his files on the Garrow case and brought out another missing persons bulletin, this one requesting information on Susan Petz's whereabouts. Placing it on his desk next to the other, Armani was struck by the physical similarities between the two girls. Alicia Hauck and Susan Petz were nearly identical in height, weight, and body frame. Carol Ann Malinowski, the girl Garrow had attempted to abduct the morning he killed Philip Domblewski, was small in stature, too. And Edith Garrow was strikingly similar in physical appearance to Alicia Hauck, Susan Petz, and Carol Ann Malinowski.

All of these women, Armani mused, greatly resembled the girl Garrow had told him about, the girlfriend the then-seventeen-year-old Garrow had walked in on while she was making love to a long-haired man, the act of betrayal from which he had attempted to flee by joining the Air Force. She was probably the first woman Garrow had been able to trust after his painfully disastrous relationship with his mother who, along with his father, had abandoned him by sending him away to work on the Maholleck farm when he was seven. By being unfaithful, the girlfriend had simply played out Garrow's developing script for women: They were untrustworthy and would always send him away or leave him. And in a man as sick as Garrow, the anger produced by such a deep-seated fear of abandonment usually led to a life of violence.

Armani also surmised that as a result of catching his girlfriend making love to the long-haired man, Garrow held any man he labeled a hippy in bitter contempt. It was even worse if, like Daniel Porter and Philip Domblewski, the man was with the type of woman to whom Garrow was sexually attracted. In that case Garrow's contempt was transformed into uncontrollable rage, in the instance of Porter and Domblewski, leading to murder.

Armani leaned back in his chair, lit a cigarette, inhaled, and winced. The Salems tasted lousy this time of day. After three packs, his mouth felt and tasted something like the insides of a charcoal brazier. Nevertheless, he took a few long drags on the cigarette, letting his gaze turn again to the two missing person bulletins on his desk. He tried to imagine what it must be like for the parents of Alicia Hauck and Susan Petz—how they must be praying for their daughters' safety, how they must be hoping against hope that their daughters would turn up alive one day soon and give this nightmare a happy ending. Armani tried to imagine the pain he and his wife would feel if one of his daughters were missing. He tried to imagine how badly he and Mary would want any news, even if the news might be that their missing daughter was dead.

He thought back to 1962, the year his younger brother, his only brother, had disappeared while flying an Air Force reconnaissance mission over the North Sea. Harry Armani's body had never been recovered. Armani remembered well the pain his parents had suffered from not knowing for certain what had happened to their son. His mother had never completely recovered from that loss. If someone even mentioned Harry's name today, some eleven years after he had gone down in the North Sea, the old woman's eyes would fill with tears.

The Garrow case was proving to be a special torment to Armani. It was pulling at him from opposite poles. Learning the details of how Garrow had killed Daniel Porter and the manner in which he had tortured, raped, and killed the Hauck and Petz girls was one thing. That was conversation on a cassette tape and had served to disgust Armani. On the other hand, finding the Boston College coed's body and now studying the photo of Alicia Hauck's remains struck a deeply personal, emotional chord within him. No matter how mentally sick Garrow might be, Armani had come to loathe the man—Robert Garrow, child molester, rapist, and sadistic killer. To Armani, Garrow represented everything reprehensible in a man.

But then there was Armani's duty as Garrow's lawyer. He was charged both by his oath as an attorney and by the law to defend his client as skillfully as possible, to do everything in his power legally to thwart the prosecution from proving Garrow guilty. If by some chance Garrow won an acquittal, that meant that Armani might have a hand in releasing a deranged murderer back into society.

With that strange and awful contradiction in mind, Armani checked his watch. He returned the missing persons bulletins to the manila folder, which he placed in the file drawer of his desk. He locked his desk and pushed out of his chair. He slipped into his raincoat and picked up his briefcase, feeling dog-tired. He had been up since seven that morning. With a plane to catch, his day was far from over.

His flight to Boston took less than an hour. He grabbed a cab at Logan Airport and was downtown a little before ten o'clock. He found the law school building and immediately noticed the single light burning on the third floor. Striding up the granite steps, he reached into his raincoat pocket and removed a slip of paper. He paused under one of the building's entry lights and checked the location of his appointment with Dean Howard Grant.* Room 311. He figured it was probably Dean Grant's light that was burning.

---

* As the details of this meeting are still privileged information, the name Dean Howard Grant and the meeting location have been changed in the account narrated here.

Armani jogged up the two flights of marble stairs to the third floor. After walking down the deserted corridor, he rapped on the wooden door marked 311.

"It's open," sounded from inside the office.

Armani let himself in. The outer office was dark. Beyond, in the private office, a green desk lamp shone over a large wooden desk. Armani walked through the reception area into a private office whose walls, except that in which the window was set, were lined from floor to ceiling with leather-bound books. Dean Howard Grant walked around from behind his desk.

"Mr. Armani. It's good to meet you." He shook Armani's hand.

"Dean Grant, thank you for seeing me."

"Please sit down." The dean motioned to the leather and wood chair facing his desk. "I just made a pot of coffee. Care for some?"

"I could use a cup, thanks," Armani answered, running a hand over the beard stubbles on his chin. "Black."

"Be right with you," Grant said as he disappeared into the reception area.

While Grant was gone from his office, Armani considered how much more impressive the law school dean looked in person than in the newspaper and magazine photos he had seen of him. In his late sixties, Grant was six-feet-four-inches tall and had a full mane of gray hair that he wore in fashionable disarray. Highlighting his angular, chiseled face were alert gray eyes and bushy salt-and-pepper eyebrows. An avid skier and hiker, Grant measured more than an ax handle across the shoulders, and his three-piece brown suit was tailored expertly around his well-tended, muscular frame. He was one of the most respected criminal lawyers in the country and had stepped out of his academic role in recent years to handle some of the most dramatic and important legal cases heard in front of the bench. A personal friend and confidante of two former U.S. presidents, Dean Grant had been called regularly to Washington to serve on various blue ribbon legal committees.

Grant returned to his office carrying a tray with two glass mugs and a sterling silver Thermos. He poured the coffee, added cream to his, then lowered himself into the chair behind his desk.

"Good flight over?"

"Not bad. We ran into a thunderstorm near Albany, and got bounced around a bit."

Grant loosened his tan and brown polka-dotted tie, then pushed a file folder to the middle of his desk. "I've read the narrative you sent me on the Garrow case," he began.

"I'm of the opinion, Dean Grant, that this could be a landmark case. I need your advice, but there is a problem."

"I assume your difficulty has to do with your note at the end of your narrative, in which you say that there are certain aspects of this case you can't divulge."

Armani instinctively reached into his pocket for a cigarette. "You mind if I smoke?"

"Feel free."

"I am privy to certain confidential information from my client. . . ."

"I see," Grant said. He withdrew a hand-carved pipe from the middle drawer of his desk. He lit it, drew deeply, and hung a cloud of blue smoke over his desk.

"This privileged information is really the crux of the issue," Armani added. "I'm just not certain how to reveal my dilemma to you so that you can give me an opinion without my breaching my client's confidentiality."

There followed a moment of silence while Grant puffed studiously on his pipe and stared at one wall of law books.

"There is one way," Grant said. "You can hire me as your attorney, thereby creating a confidentiality between us. Then you can tell me about this case."

"Hire *you* as my attorney?" Armani asked, his eyes widening.

"That's correct," Grant answered. He turned to an old Underwood manual typewriter on a stand next to his desk. He two-fingered out a brief statement, pulled the sheet of paper out of the typewriter, and handed it across the desk to Armani. It read:

> For the fee of one dollar, due and payable upon both parties signing this agreement, Frank H. Armani, Attorney at Law, engages Howard S. Grant, Doctor of Law, as his legal counsel for a period of not to exceed twenty-four hours.

Armani's face cracked into a big grin. Grant's offer to become his counsel for the next twenty-four hours for the fee of one dollar was nothing short of brilliant.

Both men signed the agreement. While Grant refilled their mugs with coffee, Armani dropped a dollar bill on the dean's desk.

"So, what is your problem?" Grant asked, sticking the dollar into his pocket.

For the next hour, Armani filled him in. Grant listened intently, taking his eyes off Armani only twice to make notes on a manila folder. When Armani finished, Grant leaned back in his chair and puffed a few times on his pipe.

"You sure got yourself a real problem with this one, didn't you?" he finally said with a smile.

"Looks that way," Armani answered. He ran his palm across his forehead to wipe away the perspiration.

"C'mon with me," Dean Grant said. He led Armani out of his office, down the corridor, and into a small computer room.

"Let's see if I can make this baby work." Grant sat in front of the terminal. He flipped on the power and began typing instructions into the computer.

The two men watched the monitor as the first line of words was spelled out: "McIntire vs. His Majesty's Court, England, 1822. Defendant (Barrister McIntire) was disbarred for breaching his client's confidence by revealing to a District Magistrate his client's heretofore undisclosed crime of murder. Disbarment upheld."

The two men waited for additional precedent cases to appear on the monitor, but none came. There was just the McIntire case.

"This *can't* be the only one," Grant said intently. He cleared the screen and once again typed the command that would retrieve the information he sought.

For a second time the McIntire case appeared alone on the monitor.

"Let's take a slightly different tack." Grant typed new instructions into the computer.

This time nine pertinent cases appeared on the monitor. They all reiterated the same basic theme. A lawyer was prohibited from divulging any evidence about his client, with two exceptions: An attorney was compelled to violate a client's confidence if divulging that information would stop a continuing crime or would prevent a future crime.

"You say your client is in custody?" Grant asked, staring at the monitor.

"Correct."

"So these particular precedent cases don't apply to your situation. There is no continuing crime, nor would your divulging the locations of the girls' bodies prevent any future crime." Grant turned the computer off and led Armani back to his office.

Once they were seated and after he had repacked and relit his pipe, the law school dean again took to staring at one wall of law books. It was as though by looking hard enough he would spot the one volume that would give them an answer.

"For whatever reason," Grant began after several moments, turning his attention back to Armani, "you've been appointed to defend a very essential tenet of American law, one that has never before been fully tested."

"A reluctant appointee," Armani answered, lighting up another Salem. "Right now I wish to hell that I never would've gotten involved with Garrow."

"Nevertheless, you've been chosen to defend this man," Grant stated, his eyes shining with the mental challenge of the issue.

Armani waited.

"You do understand that the guarantee of lawyer-client confidentiality is at stake here," Grant added. "For you to divulge the information your client has shared with you can serve as an extremely dangerous precedent to future cases."

Armani listened.

"Without the guarantee of confidentiality, no defendant would ever disclose the total information about his case to his lawyer. And you realize that the best way for any lawyer to lose a case is to know only eighty-five percent of the facts."

"I understand," Armani mumbled.

"The sacred trust that exists between a lawyer and his client must remain inviolate, at any cost."

Something about the way Grant said that made Armani wonder what that cost might end up being.

"Otherwise," Grant continued, "if a lawyer succumbed to public or police pressure to divulge what he knew about his client, our entire system of due process would be jeopardized. We simply would no longer have a true adversary system of law;

the delicate balance that exists between the prosecution and the defense would be disturbed.

"In essence, with the defense lawyer feeding information about his client to the police or to the courts, any suspect would be prosecuted not only by the people, but also by his own attorney. And make no mistake about it, Frank, without our adversary system of law, our courtrooms would resemble those in totalitarian countries, where the defense lawyer actually aids the prosecution in getting to the truth—an expediency that undercuts the much larger truth of justice. Legions of people in countries without the adversarial system of law have been jailed or executed for crimes of which they were later found innocent. Our system of law might have some faults—it may include cases such as yours that beg its shortcomings; it may even allow a few guilty people to slip out of custody because of its guarantee of due process—but I'd much rather operate under a legal system that insists on due process than one that doesn't."

"But the man is an admitted killer, a mad-dog multiple murderer!"

"Garrow still can't be forced to incriminate himself, which is exactly what happens if you disclose the locations of those girls' bodies. Plus your client is guaranteed adequate legal counsel. If you violate his confidence, Garrow isn't being provided that adequate counsel, which I know you realize is his protection under the Fifth, Sixth, Ninth, and Fourteenth Amendments to the Constitution."

"The Constitution seems to mean more to the likes of Robert Garrow then it does to law-abiding citizens," Armani commented sourly.

"If the Constitution doesn't protect the worst of us, Frank, it doesn't protect the best of us," Grant answered, sounding as though he were lecturing a first-year law student.

"And what about the parents of those girls? What do I tell them? In addition, I have no way of knowing if Garrow has killed more than the four people he's admitted murdering. There are women missing all over New York State, women who were abducted in a manner similar to Alicia Hauck. Some of these young women have been stabbed to death. . . ."

"It doesn't change anything. You're in a terrible position, one that will no doubt worsen when it finally comes out that you knew all along that Garrow killed those two girls. I don't envy your position. But I want to be clear about something, Frank. The principle for which you are standing up is one of the foundation blocks of our system of law. You cave in, and it would take years to re-establish that principle of lawyer-client confidentiality, if it could ever be fully reinstated."

"You mentioned pressure to get me to breach Garrow's confidence," Armani said, softening. "Damn, I've got state BCI agents and local cops following me wherever I go."

"As I said, I don't envy your position."

Now it was Armani's turn to stare. He looked out the window in back of Dean Grant's desk. The faint glow on the horizon over the shadowed university buildings reminded Armani how exhausted he felt.

"So I stand my ground," he finally summed up.

"I'm afraid you have no alternative," Grant said. "And if you need me at any time in the future, Frank, please call. I'll do anything I can to help you in this."

Something told Armani that, as events fully unfolded in the Garrow case, he might be in need of a top defense lawyer.

"Thank you for your time." He slowly rose from the chair, shook hands with Dean Grant, and promptly left his office.

He stepped out of the law school's doors into the cool, crisp early morning. It was quarter after six; his flight back to Syracuse didn't leave for another three hours. He paused and lit a cigarette. A couple of young men, each carrying a load of books, appeared out of the shadows. They climbed the stairs and stopped. Armani was blocking their way into the law school building.

He startled the two law students by saying, "I hope you guys know what the hell you're getting into," then stalked past the two young men and descended the stairs.

He decided to walk awhile, hoping the clean morning air would wash away some of his fear and frustration. As he made his way along the mostly deserted streets, he sorted through his feelings. There was, of course, the awful, agonizing heaviness of knowing the full truth about Robert Garrow and the distaste of defending a man whom he had come to despise. Then there was the sadness and pity he felt for the parents of Susan Petz and Alicia Hauck. He shuddered to think that the girls' parents were probably awakening about then with a constant, gnawing fear of what might have happened to their daughters.

Paradoxically, Armani was elated, too. He was excited by the legal challenge he faced. An unknown attorney with a moderately successful general law practice, he had been selected by some strange twist of circumstance to stand up for one of the most basic tenets of American law. The Garrow case would set an important precedent. Most lawyers would give their right leg for the opportunity to be so closely identified with a landmark case.

This heady, emotion-packed realization caused Armani to lighten his step and pick up his pace. He was so taken by the possibilities of the case, he didn't think about the price he might be called upon to pay before it was resolved.

14

September 1973

ARMANI PACED BACK AND FORTH across his office. He hiked
up the left sleeve of his suit jacket to check his watch—three
minutes before eleven. Three minutes before his next appointment, the inevitable confrontation he had been dreading.

His intercom buzzed. Armani leaned over his desk and depressed the speaker button.

"Mr. Petz is here to see you," his secretary's voice sounded.

"Send him right in," Armani answered. He walked quickly
around his desk and sat down in his chair. He pretended to be
reading something as the door to his office pushed open and the
father of one of the murdered girls walked through the doorway.

"Mr. Petz, I'm Frank Armani. He stood up to shake hands
with the other man. "It's nice to meet you." After a moment of
awkward silence, Armani added, "Please, sit down."

Petz settled into the chair facing the lawyer's desk. Armani
sat back down, folded his hands on his green blotter, and
looked closely at the man facing him. Daniel Petz was a high-
ranking executive with a midwestern insurance company. At-
tired in an expensively tailored, three-piece blue suit, he was
handsome, with brooding blue eyes and well-groomed brown
hair that was frosted at the temples.

"I've traveled from Chicago to inquire about my daughter,
Mr. Armani," Petz began.

Armani reached for a cigarette. As he pulled his lighter away from the cigarette, he hoped that Petz hadn't noticed that his hand was shaking.

"I'd like to know if you have any information as to Susan's whereabouts," Petz added in a mannered, pleading tone, ". . . whether Mr. Garrow told you what he's done with my daughter."

"First of all," Armani began, choosing his words carefully, "let me say that I'm very sorry about what you're going through. I have daughters of my own and can imagine something of the anguish you and your wife have suffered over your daughter's disappearance. But I must make one thing very clear. My client is only a suspect in your daughter's disappearance. Robert Garrow hasn't been charged with any crimes having to do with Susan's abduction."

"The newspapers have been filled with stories about how Garrow might be involved with my daughter's disappearance," Petz replied, ". . . about how the police are preparing a case against Garrow in the matter."

"The media and the police can say anything they care to," Armani clarified, making a special effort to be gentle. The man had been through enough without being treated brusquely by him. "But the fact remains that the police have no case against my client for any crimes relating to your daughter's disappearance. If they had, they would've asked for an indictment, as they have done in the Philip Domblewski killing."

"Can you tell me anything?" Petz pleaded. "My wife and I have exhausted every other possible source of information." He removed his handkerchief from his pants pocket and dabbed at his eyes. "Should we keep hoping . . . and praying?" Tears accented his words.

Armani searched his mind for some phrase, some small shred of information he could convey that might help ease the man's grief. Then he remembered Dean Grant's warning about being charged by the law and by his ethics as a lawyer not to disclose anything he had learned from his client.

"As I said, I am very sorry that this terrible thing has happened to you," Armani hedged, feeling small and cowardly for doing so. "I know how difficult all this must be for you and for your wife."

He thought for a moment about relating the story of his

brother's disappearance eleven years earlier over the North At-
lantic, of telling how his parents and he himself went through
hell from not ever knowing for certain what had happened. But
he dismissed the idea. He didn't wish to come off sounding any
more patronizing or solicitous than he already had.

"So you have no information to share with me about
Susan?" Petz asked.

"All I can say to you right now, Mr. Petz, is that my co-
counsel on this case and I are meeting tomorrow with the State
Bureau of Criminal Investigation and with the Hamilton
County district attorney. Something could come out of that
conference that I'll be able to share with you."

"What sort of conference?" Petz pressed.

"I can't tell you that," Armani answered. "But you have my
word that if something comes out of our meeting tomorrow, I'll
let you know immediately."

"That's good enough for me," Petz said. "I'll be staying at
the Hotel Syracuse."

"I'll be in touch with you right after tomorrow's conference."
Armani walked Petz to the door.

After Petz had stepped out of the office, Armani walked back
to his desk. He stood for a few moments and stared blankly out
of his office window. He watched the fearful, anxious Mr. Petz
climb into a late model sedan and drive away. In a sudden response to the frustration he felt, Armani grabbed a heavy legal
volume from his desk and threw it against the far wall of his
office. Then, in a frenzy, he raked his arm across the desk and
swept pens, pencils, a pair of glasses, and about twenty file folders full of papers onto the floor.

His secretary stuck her head into his office. "Is there something wrong, Mr. Armani?"

Standing rigid in the middle of the room, his fists balled at
his sides, Armani muttered, "Just everything, Sharon. Everything is wrong."

The middle-aged woman was about to retreat out of his office to leave Armani alone with his anger when he added,
"Sharon, if either Mr. or Mrs. Hauck should call, asking to see
me . . ."

His secretary prompted him to finish the statement. "I
should tell them . . . ?"

". . . that I'm unavailable; I'm out of town . . . anything. Just take the message."

"Certainly, Mr. Armani."

She turned and was closing the door to his office when she heard him add, "I can't face them. I just can't face them."

15

That Night

MARY WAS IN BED next to him. She was asleep and snoring; the covers rose and fell with each breath she drew. Armani lay awake, staring through the pale wash of moonlight at the ceiling, replaying the scene of the previous morning in his office. He couldn't get the image of the fearfully expectant, pleading Daniel Petz out of his mind. He turned his head to read the luminous dial on the alarm clock next to his bed. Three-thirty. Once again he closed his eyes in search of sleep. This time he got lucky and drifted off, only to experience a frighteningly clear and realistic dream.

Susan Petz was lying alone in the airshaft of the abandoned mine near Mineville. Her eyebrows and close-cropped hair were frosted over from the cold air that rushed from deep within the earth; she appeared to be sleeping. Then, quietly and slowly, Susan Petz stirred, awaking from her death sleep. She began whimpering for someone to rescue her from her frigid resting place. Above her, at ground level and staring down into the airshaft at her, was Frank Armani. He ignored her pleas, turning instead to Robert Garrow, who was standing next to him at the edge of the airshaft. He put his arm around Garrow's shoulders, and the two men walked away. As they did, he said, "It's okay, Bob. She's only the victim. You're the client. . . ."

Armani bolted straight up in bed. He was wringing wet, and

the bedsheets were rancid from his perspiration. He pushed himself quietly from bed and slipped on his robe.

Mary's sleep-clotted voice sounded. "You all right, Frank?"

"Yeah, I'm okay. Go back to sleep, Mary. I'm going downstairs for a few minutes."

"Anything I can do?" she asked.

"No, nothing."

He left their bedroom. On his way downstairs, something impelled him to look in on his daughters. He wanted to be certain they were safe. Seeing that they were quietly asleep, Armani headed down the stairs and into the kitchen. He made himself a cup of instant coffee, lit a cigarette, and read the evening paper for the second time. It went on like that for the rest of the night—he drank coffee, lit one cigarette off the other, and studied the newspaper until morning appeared through the slider window that looked out on the backyard. Exhausted, he climbed the stairs to the bathroom and showered. After dressing quietly so he wouldn't wake Mary, he carried his shoes back down to the kitchen, where he made himself another cup of coffee, lit another Salem, and watched for the morning paper.

16

The Following Morning

Armani sat at his desk, studying the fan of papers spread out in front of him. Feeling clammy and irritable, he was in shirtsleeves, and his tie was pulled loose from his throat. When he finished reading the typewritten statement, he leaned back in his chair, sighed deeply, and stared at Francis Belge, who was standing alongside him.

"What do you think?" Belge asked carefully.

"I think this entire idea is nuts."

"This *case* is nuts."

"They're never going to go for this," Armani said, jabbing his lighted cigarette at the papers on his desk.

"Look, Frank, we owe it to our client to attempt to plea bargain his case. It was his idea—"

"His idea! C'mon, for cryin' out loud." Armani stood up. "You went up to the hospital and cooked this thing up with him? Garrow doesn't have the sense for anything like this."

"Okay, so I agreed with Garrow that plea bargaining his case was his best shot."

"You had no right to go behind my back and talk with Garrow," Armani said, his temples and forehead reddening.

"Frank, we don't have time to argue this right now. Intemann and McCabe are due here any minute. I say it's our job to do the best thing for our client."

"You say? What about me, dammit? Don't I have any say in this thing?"

Armani's annoyance with Belge had begun with learning that his co-counsel had taken it upon himself to enlist Ralph Kackison's aid in locating Alicia Hauck's body in Oakwood Cemetery. Since then, he had come to suspect that Belge was attempting to take the lead away from him in the Garrow case. It was Belge who had scheduled today's plea bargaining conference with Hamilton County District Attorney William Intemann and BCI Investigator Henry McCabe.

"Of course you have something to say about this," Belge answered, softening. "I don't know what the big deal is. All along you've agreed that Garrow is nuttier than a fruitcake. If we can get the DA to go along with the fact today, we save the trial. And we both realize that we're being set up to be screwed on this case. The Hamilton County DA knows *everyone* in that county—they're all bass fishing buddies up there. You can bet that he'll have the jurors in his pocket before the opening gavel drops. The entire county wants Garrow to fry, as evidenced by the fact that they wouldn't hear of a change of venue at the arraignment. To top it off, Garrow gets judged sane to stand trial as a result of the court-appointed psychiatrist's report.

"C'mon, Frank. You know this plea bargaining session is probably our first and last chance to avoid a kangaroo court trial for our client."

Armani continued glaring at him.

"Besides," Belge added in his best conciliatory tone, "you're just angry because, for the sake of expediency, I arranged this thing with Garrow directly and didn't include you."

Armani had to admit that much of his resistance to the plea bargaining tactic *did* have to do with Belge's going behind his back to arrange the terms of the agreement. In truth, Armani himself had figured to plea bargain all along. He just would have preferred Belge to be up front about things, so they could both have had a hand in drawing up the agreement. But even that point, Armani had to admit to himself, was no big deal. There wasn't much leeway on the terms. They only had certain items with which to bargain.

Armani's intercom buzzed.

"What ticks me off most," Armani said, keeping his eyes on

Belge as he reached for the intercom box, "is that you waited until now to let me read this document."

"What can I say?" Belge gave Armani a coy, guilty look. "My secretary only finished typing up the document a few minutes ago."

Armani shook his head. He knew better than to believe that one.

"Yeah?" Armani said into the intercom.

"Misters McCabe and Intemann are here to see you," Sharon announced.

"Send them in," he responded. He turned the papers over on his desk, so they couldn't be read by Intemann or McCabe.

"Remember, Frank," Belge added quickly. "Nothing about the bodies until they agree to our terms. Those are Garrow's orders."

"Yeah, yeah," Armani answered. He tightened his tie, slipped on his suit jacket, and watched his office door swing open.

"Henry," Armani said, taking McCabe's hand. "You know Francis Belge?"

"Haven't had the pleasure." The tall, lean investigator shook Belge's hand.

The two lawyers then greeted William Intemann, the thirty-seven-year-old Hamilton County district attorney. Dressed in a blue polyester suit, Intemann stood eye-to-eye with Armani. His head seemed too large for his rounded shoulders and abbreviated neck. He had thin lips and a straight, prominent nose. He wore his brown hair cut fairly short, yet allowed his sideburns to grow well down his cheeks. As a district attorney from a rural, sparsely populated county, Intemann had the opportunity to show his talents as a prosecutor on the Garrow case, the first murder trial in Hamilton County since 1929.

Once Intemann and McCabe were seated, Belge hoisted himself up on the front edge of his co-counsel's desk. Armani had to keep himself from smiling. That was pure Francis Belge, placing himself in the position of looking down at his adveraries, so that he had the tactical advantage.

"Okay," Belge began. "Let's first understand one another. If these plea bargaining negotiations break down, nothing revealed by our side today can be used against us in court. It's all confidential and privileged information."

"Understood," Intemann acknowledged. Keeping confidential the information revealed in a plea bargaining session was the unwritten rule. Otherwise no defense attorney would ever tip his hand in these proceedings, for fear that his bargaining information would be used later in the courtroom against his client.

Armani glanced across at Intemann and McCabe. Of the two, the BCI investigator seemed the more relaxed. He sat cross-legged in the chair and, with a practiced nonchalance, flicked the ashes off his cigarette into Armani's wastepaper basket. Intemann, on the other hand, had his arms crossed over his chest, and the muscles in his jaw were tensed. Armani figured that Intemann had heard about Belge's wily brilliance as a criminal lawyer and was nervous about negotiating with him.

Belge looked down at the BCI investigator and said, "We might be able to help you close your files on several unsolved homicides, McCabe."

McCabe's eyebrows arched, but he said nothing.

"Plus," Belge continued, turning his eyes to Intemann, "We can save the people of Hamilton County the several hundred thousand dollars they will have to spend to prosecute Garrow for the Domblewski killing."

Armani's eyes narrowed with satisfaction. He knew that Hamilton County, with only forty-seven hundred residents, could ill afford the cost of the Garrow trial. Score one for Belge.

Belge continued, "In trade for the information that will allow you to close your files on the unsolved homicides to which I'm referring, along with avoiding the prohibitively costly trial, we want certain concessions for our client."

"Those concessions are?" McCabe asked.

"Reduction of charges against Garrow for killing Philip Domblewski to manslaughter first degree, based on insanity," Belge explained, shifting his attention from McCabe to Intemann. "Plus an insanity judgment on any other charges that might be filed against him now and in the future, including the felony counts resulting from the charges against him in Syracuse for sexually molesting those two young girls last June."

"We have no jurisdiction to bargain the Onondaga County charges." Intemann was working hard to retain his attitude of rigid indifference.

"We realize that," Belge said. "But I'm certain that if you go along, we can get the Onondaga County DA to agree."

"Why should we give away the Porter murder?" McCabe asked, playing thoughtfully with his chin. "Who's to say that we don't have enough on your boy to convict him on that one?"

Belge had a twinkle in his eyes as he answered. "Considering that another murder indictment against Garrow at this time would immeasurably help you in getting a conviction in the Domblewski trial, you would have charged him by now if you had enough on him for the Porter murder."

Henry McCabe's face softened. Belge had called his bluff. The Bureau of Criminal Investigation hadn't been able to put together enough proof in the Porter case to ask for an indictment against Garrow.

"I've got one problem with your terms," McCabe countered. "Garrow isn't insane. A sex pervert, yeah. But he's not insane. The reason he killed Domblewski was to get rid of any witnesses to his planned abduction of the Malinowski girl. If that one kid hadn't escaped and brought help from Wells, Garrow would've killed all three of those guys rather than risk going back to jail."

"If your thesis is right, Henry," Belge said, "why didn't Garrow kill those little girls in Syracuse he abducted and sexually molested?"

McCabe had no reply.

"What we're doing here," Belge continued, "is offering you a hedge against the shrinks' finding Garrow loony enough that a jury goes for our 'innocent by reason of insanity' plea. If we win in court, according to the law, Garrow goes to a mental institution *only* for as long as he's considered insane. After that, he's a free man. Then you know what you have? The most feared man in New York State on the streets, and nothing on those other unsolved homicides except a file full of inconclusive garbage. Stack that possibility against a solution on those other homicides, an avoidance of a costly jury trial, and Garrow gets put away in a mental institution for the rest of his life."

"Garrow has agreed to those terms?" McCabe asked.

"He has," Belge responded.

Armani could see another reason for Intemann and McCabe to plea bargain this case: If this thing went to trial, Belge was going to make William Intemann look inept. There was a good chance that Belge would walk Garrow right out of the courtroom.

"How do you propose to solve these open homicides?" Intemann asked.

Belge's eyes lit up again. This time it was because he smelled a trap. "Let's just say that we can direct you to where some bodies are hidden."

"Does that mean that Alicia Hauck and Susan Petz are dead and not just missing?" McCabe asked.

"No comment," Belge said straight-faced, "until you agree to our terms."

"What about that map we found in his car?" McCabe pressed. "The one with the dots and women's first names spread all over the state. We figure Garrow had something to do with at least twenty-seven murders and rapes. You gonna clear those up for us?"

"Again, no comment until you agree to our terms," Belge reiterated.

Intemann's lips turned white and bloodless, and his head began shaking. "I have to say that we are outraged that you would even consider trading information on the bodies of Alicia Hauck and Susan Petz to extract a deal for a cold-blooded killer."

"We've never acknowledged that our information has to do with Susan Petz or Alicia Hauck," Belge stated. "And *if* they are dead, there is nothing any of us can do to bring them back to life."

"That has nothing to do with it, and you know it," Intemann countered, his voice trembling with fury. "And I'm telling you that if you know the locations of those bodies and haven't informed the police, I'll seek criminal charges against you and Armani for withholding evidence and for obstructing justice."

"C'mon, Bill," Belge said, "you've got no legal basis to do anything like that."

"We'll see," Intemann threatened. "We'll see."

"Am I to take it, then," Belge summed up, "that you're rejecting our offer?"

"Exactly," Intemann answered tersely. "Your offer is rejected. Totally. We're going for a murder conviction."

The four men traded glances. Intemann got to his feet. "I want to add that I think your conduct in this matter is totally unethical. I am outraged."

"I believe we understand how you feel," Belge completed, lowering himself from the edge of Armani's desk so that he stood facing the Hamilton County district attorney. "We're simply trying to save everyone involved further grief and expense. The Garrow trial could drag on for months. It'll absorb all of your energies, Bill. As a one-man district attorney's office, I'm certain you have other matters that demand your attention."

"You haven't heard?" Intemann asked, his face softening into a smile.

"What's that?"

"Owing to the fact that my office's resources are limited, Onondaga County has agreed to assign one of their assistant district attorneys to act as my co-prosecutor on this case."

Belge's eyebrows arched with surprise. With the powerful Onondaga county district attorney's office entering the case, he was losing an advantage on which he had counted heavily, one of the few afforded him in the Garrow case. He had been looking forward to competing against a small-time district attorney, a lawyer with limited research facilities and no experience trying a murder case. Onondaga County Chief Prosecutor Jon Holcombe was a real law-and-order man, one who went for the maximum penalty on almost every case he tried. That helped explain the reason for Intemann's hard-line stance in refusing the plea bargaining attempt. It was Holcombe as much as Intemann who had done the talking this afternoon in Armani's office.

"One more thing," Belge added as McCabe and Intemann were preparing to leave. "We'd appreciate it if you'd call off your dogs and quit trailing us. Not only is it a waste of the taxpayers' money, it's illegal. You keep following us or continue listening in on our conversations with Garrow, and I'm going to ask for a mistrial based on your preventing us from properly defending our client."

McCabe straightened his tie. "Off the record, we haven't been tailing Armani. Just you, Belge," he said.

"Just me?" Belge asked.

"Let's say that we're figuring you would try anything to spring Garrow." McCabe smiled and turned for the door.

Armani and Belge both knew that, with the Onondaga County District Attorney's office participating in the case, they were in for a real dog fight. The prosecution was bringing in the big guns to get Robert Garrow. And Intemann's warning—that if Belge and Armani knew the locations of the Hauck and Petz bodies, he would seek to prosecute the two defense attorneys—made it clear that they were risking possible disbarment. Both men understood that the ante to defend Garrow had been raised as a result of this afternoon's plea bargaining session.

For his part, Armani didn't need to look to the future for problems. There were enough of them staring him in the face now.

First, he completed the unenviable task of calling Susan Petz's father to explain that he could offer him no further information about his daughter's fate. Beyond that, and more significant to preparing Garrow's defense, Armani realized that he was in danger of losing control of the case. Belge was trying to take over as head of the defense team. The realization frustrated and angered Armani. This was *his* case, not Belge's.

In the weeks following the unsuccessful plea bargaining attempt, Armani's law offices were broken into three times. The intruders, gaining entrance each time by jimmying the front door, took nothing—none of the easily fenced computer equipment or electronic typewriters, nor the one hundred dollars in petty cash Armani's secretary kept in her unlocked desk drawer. The only item tampered with was Armani's file cabinet. It was gone through in such a professional manner that Armani only realized that his files had been rifled when he discovered certain key folders out of sequence in the drawer.

However, having expected the authorities to go to any lengths to make a case against Garrow in the Hauck, Petz, and Porter homicides, Armani was one step ahead of the intruders. He had carefully hidden the photographs of the bodies and the cassette tapes of Garrow's confession in the basement of his father's house in Solvay. Even at that, once his office had been broken into, Armani became increasingly uncomfortable with the existence of the photographs and cassette tapes. He reasoned that if they were bold enough to ransack his office, they might somehow get a judge to subpoena his records on the case. If this happened, Armani would face another difficult decision: Should he perjure himself and say that they didn't exist, to protect himself and his client? Or should he surrender the tapes and photographs, thereby breaching Garrow's confidentiality?

After agonizing over the various possibilities, he drove to his father's house, retrieved the photos and cassette tapes from the basement, and burned them.

17

Winter 1973–1974

THE MASSIVE AMOUNT of work Armani had to perform to prepare for the Garrow trial left him no time for his other clients. He was forced to turn over the balance of his open cases to the other three attorneys in his firm.

His exhaustive twelve- to fourteen-hour-a-day work schedule took its toll in other areas of his life. An avid skier, Armani had to be content to let the dust build up on his downhill equipment. He endured a rash of colds and extended bouts of the flu. And, whether resulting from his secret knowledge of the fate of Alicia Hauck and Susan Petz or from long days and nights spent at his desk or on the road talking to potential witnesses, interviewing psychiatrists and interrogating Garrow, Armani's insomnia worsened. Nights on end he would lie awake next to Mary or sit at their kitchen table smoking cigarettes and drinking coffee until the sun rose.

There was another, potentially disastrous side effect of his efforts at constructing an impregnable defense for Garrow. A hard drinker in his younger days, Armani had given the stuff up several years earlier after realizing that alcohol was causing him serious difficulties at home and in his law practice. Now, to combat his fatigue and frustrations, Armani began using alcohol again. It was nothing heavy, but he was finding that a couple of scotches late in the afternoon relaxed him enough so that he could work far into the night.

115

Mary Armani didn't like what she was seeing. Her husband's resurrected drinking habit reawakened the deep, bitter resentments she had carried during her husband's riotous, bar-crawling, skirt-chasing years. The couple had separated during that stormy phase of their marriage, to reconcile only after Frank had quit drinking and stayed closer to home. But now, with her husband back to drinking again and staying away from home for several days at a time rummaging around northern New York looking for witnesses and evidence with Francis Belge, Mary was afraid Frank might fall back into his old ways. In truth, she feared her husband's association with Belge as much as she did Frank's drinking. It wasn't that she disliked Belge; she was actually fond of the man. Mary just knew that the tall, good-looking lawyer was a notorious drinker and womanizer. As far as Mary Armani was concerned, the more time her husband spent with Belge, the greater the chance of his getting into extramarital, boozy scrapes. So Mary reacted the only way she knew: She began putting pressure on her husband to spend more time at home and to take a more active role in raising their daughters.

Armani was in a trap. If Garrow was to be provided a proper insanity defense, Frank Armani would have to put in the time to construct it. Belge wasn't much help in that area. He was a great trial lawyer, but he shied away from the meticulous, back-breaking research that was so necessary now. If Armani didn't do the preparations, didn't solidly lay the foundation for the insanity defense, he knew it wouldn't get done.

He tried to explain to Mary that this wasn't the kind of case on which he could close the file each day and be home at six o'clock for dinner, in time to spend a quiet evening in front of the television with his family. He tried to make her understand that this was his big one—this was the case that was going to forge his reputation as a top-flight criminal lawyer. After this one, he reasoned, people were going to be seeking him out from all over the country to defend them.

But Mary saw it a different way. Not only did she consider him consumed with building an airtight defense for his client, she also saw him as hooked on the publicity afforded him as the attorney for one of the most feared killers in New York State history. He seemed to enjoy thoroughly the unending string of interviews with newspaper, radio, and television reporters. Even though he constantly complained to her that the interviews were bothersome and time-consuming, it was evident to Mary that her husband was addicted to all of the attention.

18

December 1973

Robert Morrison, a Syracuse University student, was cutting through Oakwood Cemetery on a rainy December afternoon when he spotted what appeared to be the remains of a human body in the denuded underbrush near the cemetery's maintenance building. He immediately notified the police, who, by checking dental records, positively identified the remains as those of Alicia Hauck, the sixteen-year-old girl missing since the previous July. They also ascertained that the girl had been strangled to death, then stabbed repeatedly, as if her killer had attempted to torture her corpse. Her body was too badly decomposed to determine if she had been sexually molested before she was murdered.

Though careful to state that they had no specific evidence to tie him to the murder, Syracuse police investigators announced to the press that they wanted to question Robert Garrow about the death of Alicia Hauck.

Less than two weeks after Alicia Hauck's body was discovered, a group of school kids playing in the Barton Hill area of Mineville spotted what appeared to be a human foot protruding from some debris in the airshaft of the old Republic Steel mine. They reported their findings to their teacher, who called the sheriff. The following day, a team consisting of members of the sheriff's department and the Bureau of Criminal Investigation and headed by Senior BCI Investigator Henry McCabe retrieved the body of a young female. By comparing dental records, the BCI determined that they had found the remains of Susan Petz, the twenty-year-old Boston College coed missing since mid-June. She had been stabbed repeatedly in the chest and had been beaten on the head with a blunt object.

Henry McCabe announced to the media that, although there was strong circumstantial evidence linking Robert Garrow to the Petz killing, no indictment against Garrow would be sought at this time, pending completion of the BCI's investigation into the young coed's murder.

The discovery of the bodies of Alicia Hauck and Susan Petz brought a tragic ending to their parents' long, agonizing ordeal.

19

May 1974

FRANK ARMANI, with Francis Belge in the passenger seat, pulled his Mercedes into the crowded parking lot of the Hamilton County courthouse in Lake Pleasant. A throng of radio, television, and newspaper reporters milled around the brick archway connecting the courthouse to the jail.

"Will you look at that?" Armani cried when he spotted the reporters.

Belge said nothing. He simply turned and plucked his briefcase from the backseat.

Armani climbed out from behind the steering wheel and walked around to the back of his car. He removed his briefcase and three grocery bags full of data from the trunk.

The two lawyers had taken but a couple of steps toward the courthouse when they were recognized. In seconds they were surrounded by a crowd of reporters, who began snapping pictures and firing questions.

Armani turned to his co-counsel and grinned widely. "This is the big time, Belge. Didn't I tell you, dammit?"

"Let's just get the hell inside," Belge answered tersely.

Their route to the door was blocked. One of the reporters, the gray-haired *New York Times* correspondent, asked, "How are you guys going to handle Garrow's defense?"

Belge paused and measured the man with his eyes. "As skillfully as possible."

"C'mon," the reporter persisted. "Give us something, will-ya?"

"Mr. Armani and I have to attend a pretrial meeting right now. Maybe we'll have something for you when we're done." His face illuminated by a barrage of flashbulbs, Belge offered a sly grin.

The two lawyers pushed through the crush of newspeople, and entered the back door of the courthouse. Once out of ear-shot of the guard at the door, Armani asked, "You really going to talk to those reporters after the pretrial conference?"

"Naw," Belge answered. "Just like to keep 'em sucking. That way they'll be primed when we do want to slide something into the media that'll benefit us."

Armani shook his head. Struggling with his paper bags full of material, he followed Belge into a small, deserted courtroom whose wooden benches were designed to hold a maximum of fifty people. The two lawyers walked around the raised judge's bench and paused at the single wooden door set in the court-room's far wall. Belge turned the knob and walked right in.

Judge Marthen was seated on one corner of the conference table. He was wearing a loose-fitting blue suit and smoking a cigarette. Three other men were in the room. There was William Intemann, the Hamilton County district attorney, and, seated behind Judge Marthen, Norman Mordue, assigned by the newly appointed Onondaga District Attorney, Jon Hol-combe, to serve as co-prosecutor in the trial. The third man was hunched over a court stenographer's machine.

"Gentlemen," Judge Marthen spoke, "I'm sure you both know Mr. Mordue."

Moving to shake hands with Belge and Armani, Mordue walked with a distinct limp, the result of a combat injury he had suffered while serving in Vietnam. A former Syracuse University star halfback, the ruggedly built co-prosecutor wore his neatly cut hair combed to one side. He had a round, boyish face, and intense brown eyes. Neither Belge nor Armani had ever come up against Mordue in a courtroom before, but they knew of him as a competent, aggressive prosecutor.

"I guess we can get under way," Marthen said, once the law-yers were seated.

As Marthen settled his backside on the conference table again, Armani found himself wondering how the judge would handle Belge's unusual courtroom antics once the trial started. Belge thrived on intimidating a judge; he was the Billy Martin of the legal game. And from what Armani had learned, Marthen prided himself on not being bullied by any lawyer trying a case in front of him.

Marthen's opening statement to the defense and prosecution teams gave Armani a solid hint of what was to come in the courtroom. The judge was evidently well acquainted with Belge's reputation.

"Let me say first off, gentlemen," Marthen said, his brown eyes moving in a hawklike fashion between the quartet of lawyers, "that during this trial there is going to be only one bastard in my courtroom. And *I'm* going to be that bastard. Is that understood?"

"No objection, your honor," Belge answered, flashing a sheepish smile.

Armani, Intemann, and Mordue acknowledged the judge's remark in turn.

"Now that's understood, we can move along with the business at hand," Marthen continued. "A couple of preliminary matters. First, because of the courtroom's limited seating capacity, I will allow only three news reporters to sit in on the jury selection process."

"There's an army of them out there, your honor," Intemann offered.

"I realize that," Marthen explained. "They've agreed to select a pool of three reporters who will provide the rest with notes of each day's proceeding during the jury selection." He paused to light another cigarette. "Next, I have decided to make everything we do here a matter of court record. There will always be two court reporters present during the trial. Doug here will take down what is said in chambers. I want this trial to go in clear and clean, and I want nothing left out."

"Will we be getting daily copies of the transcript?" Belge asked.

"Each evening a complete set of the dailies will be delivered to the defense and prosecution teams for your study before the next day's proceedings."

Belge nodded his agreement.

"I'm going to have to ask, Mr. Belge, that you give your responses verbally. While it's not so important here in my chambers, as the court reporter can see you, in the courtroom, with everything that'll be going on, the reporters may not be able to see your nod."

"Yes, your honor," Belge answered. "I go on record as agreeing with your plan of delivering the dailies of each day's proceedings to our hotel each night."

"As I do," Intemann ratified.

"All right," Marthen continued. "I have also decided to sequester the jury so they won't be influenced by any inflammatory news reports."

"Speaking of that," Belge interjected, pulling a newspaper out of his briefcase, "this paper carried a feature article based on remarks District Attorney Intemann made a month ago about this trial. The article is highly prejudicial to my client, and I move for a mistrial."

"That article has already been introduced as evidence in the appellate court," Intemann answered quickly, "on the occasion of Mr. Armani's petition for a change of venue. In turning down the defense request for a change of venue, the appellate court also rejected Mr. Armani's motion for a mistrial based on this article. Therefore, it shouldn't be allowed to be introduced here—"

"I will rule on the law, Mr. Intemann," Marthen cut in. "I deny Mr. Belge's request for a mistrial."

"Exception, your honor," Belge said.

"Exception noted," the judge answered.

"Regarding sequestering the jury," Belge picked up. "I assume they will be sequestered as they are selected, one at a time."

"That is not my plan, Mr. Belge. Sequestering each juror as they are picked will place an undue hardship on those who serve. As it is, this trial could last several weeks. That will be hardship enough on these people."

"Exception, your honor," Belge challenged, "based on the fact that each juror, as he or she waits for the full jury to be selected, will run the risk of being prejudiced by inflammatory news stories about the trial."

"Exception noted," Marthen said.

It went on like that for the next hour. In an attempt to gain seemingly insignificant advantages that might profit him during the trial, Belge challenged each of Judge Marthen's procedural points. For his part, Marthen, though never knuckling under to Belge's challenges, ruled fairly. When one of Belge's requests made sense, such as the one to allow Garrow to be brought unshackled each morning from the jail to the courthouse—the suspect was hardly an escape risk, Belge maintained, since he was still confined to a wheelchair from wounds suffered when captured—Marthen changed his mind and ruled in Belge's favor.

"Okay," Marthen said in conclusion. "I have every confidence that we're going to have a fair and expeditious trial. I have the highest respect for each member of the defense and prosecution teams. You are all very capable and qualified officers of the court. Now, let's get a jury selected and get on with the trial."

With that the pretrial meeting broke up.

Belge and Armani walked next door to the jail for a conference with their client. Though the first floor of the Hamilton County jail had been designed to hold five male prisoners, there were only four in lockup. The cell next to Garrow's was vacant for security reasons.

When his lawyers arrived, Garrow was seated in a wheelchair next to the cot in his cramped cell. His left arm was still in a sling. It was withered, no bigger around than a zucchini squash. His left foot, still in a cast, was held straight out by one of the wheelchair's extension stanchions.

As he had been during most of the dozens of sessions he had had with his attorneys since confessing to Belge last August about the Hauck, Petz, and Porter killings, Garrow was cooperative and helpful. He answered his attorneys' questions the best he could but stuck to his story about not remembering the exact details of the murders. It was as though he had blocked out forever from his conscious mind the precise moments he had killed Daniel Porter, Susan Petz, Alicia Hauck, and Philip Domblewski. If Armani had any criticism of Garrow since the suspect had turned cooperative, it was that he had summoned his attorney to Champlain Valley Physicians Hospital or, since the preceding September, to the Hamilton County jail at least four times a week. Over the past nine months, it seemed to Armani that he had spent the major portion of his time driving to either Plattsburgh or Lake Pleasant to confer with his client about mostly insignificant details relating to the upcoming trial.

Because Hamilton County was so sparsely populated, everyone involved with the trial figured it would be difficult to pick an unbiased jury of twelve plus two alternates. But no one thought it would be as difficult as it worked out to be. Over the next four weeks, from May 8th to June 10th, twenty-five hundred out of the thirty-two hundred people in the county eligible for jury duty were screened. It was an exhausting, nerve-fraying process in which most were disqualified for already having formed an opinion as to the guilt of Robert Garrow, for being close acquaintances of District Attorney Intemann or Judge George Marthen, or for having extenuating family and business reasons for not serving. (Since it was the beginning of tourist season—tourism was Hamilton County's largest industry—many people begged off serving on the jury for the reason that doing so would create a severe economic hardship on them.)

During the month-long jury selection process, Belge exhibited his brilliance in ferreting out crucial information from prospective jurors. He successfully saw to it that dozens of people who claimed an inability to consider an "innocent by reason of insanity" verdict were disqualified. He did this by means of direct questioning or by less orthodox means. One ploy involved Donna, the blonde who had helped Belge and Armani shake their police tail the previous August when the two lawyers were searching for the body of Susan Petz.

Armani was surprised to learn that Donna wasn't of Scandinavian extraction. Rather, she was deaf. Having never heard the spoken word and unable to repeat the language precisely, the woman had developed her accent from learning to speak and comprehend by reading lips, a skill Belge used wisely during the jury selection process. Unknown to Intemann and Mordue, the blond woman watched them closely as they privately discussed the merits of prospective jurors at the prosecutor's table. During recess, Donna reported back to Belge what she had learned by reading the lips of the prosecuting attorneys.

Once court resumed, Belge enraged Intemann by asking that the person Donna had indicated might be sympathetic to the prosecution be excused from jury duty.

On June 10th the announcement was made that a jury had been selected. The average age of those who would decide the defendant's guilt or innocence was 62.5 years old—hardly, Belge maintained loudly to the press, a jury of Robert Garrow's peers.

20

June 1974

DURING THE JURY SELECTION PROCESS, Armani commuted home each weekend from Lake Pleasant. He spent Saturdays and Sundays in his office going through the previous week's trial transcripts and reviewing his extensive files on Garrow in preparation for the upcoming week in the courtroom. Sunday evening he left Syracuse for Lake Pleasant, stopping on the way through Rome to eat dinner at Matt Latich's Restaurant. The lawyer had known Latich since the early sixties.

On Sunday, June 12th, Latich was standing in his customary position behind the bar when Armani entered the restaurant. Latich's jolly, fleshy face was usually highlighted by mischievous green eyes, but this night his face and eyes didn't reveal much joy.

"How's it going, counselor?" Latich asked as Armani approached the bar.

"Going," a weary Armani answered. "Gimme a Black Label, will you, Matt?"

Latich reached into the cooler under the bar for a frosty bottle of Carling Black Label and placed it, along with a glass, on the bar.

"See by the papers that you finally got a jury," Latich offered. He brought the Sunday paper out from under the bar. The headlines read: GARROW JURY SET. And in smaller type: TRIAL BEGINS THIS WEEK.

"Finally," Armani answered, sipping the beer. Still not comfortable drinking in his home, Armani looked forward to having a few at Latich's each Sunday evening.

Latich stared at Armani for a few long seconds with a look that unnerved the lawyer.

"What the hell's the matter with you?" Armani asked. "You just been held up or something?"

Latich glanced each way down the bar. Satisfied the other half dozen patrons were busily engaged in conversations of their own, he leaned over the bar until his face was only inches from Armani's.

"I had some visitors here yesterday, Frank," Latich said, holding his voice low. "Guys from the eastern part of the state."

"So you're telling me that you draw clientele from all over the state." Armani smiled. "Always knew you ran a popular joint."

"It's no joke, Frank," Latich interjected anxiously. "Those guys were in here looking for someone to honor a contract."

Armani put his glass down on the bar.

"And you know whose names are on that contract? Yours and Belge's."

"What the hell are you talking about, Matt?"

"I swear to you. They were looking for someone to take you guys out."

"Who the hell are *they*?" an astonished Armani asked.

"Can't tell you that. All I know for sure is that they have a real strong interest in seeing that your client hangs."

"Garrow?"

"That's right," Latich answered, wiping the bar.

"Why the hell . . . ?"

"Because they figure you're going to get him off on the insanity gig."

"You gotta be kidding," Armani answered.

"Just watch your ass, that's all, counselor," Latich finished. "And don't let on where you heard the news, willya? I don't need any trouble."

"Don't worry," Armani said. He watched Latich walk down to the other end of the bar, where someone was asking for a refill on his drink.

No longer feeling hungry, Armani finished his beer and left the restaurant.

En route to Lake Pleasant, Armani didn't know what to think about Latich's warning. It seemed so preposterous that anyone, even a couple of extremist law-and-order nuts, would want to kill the attorneys defending the man suspected of murder. Maybe try and eliminate Garrow, yes. But why carry out a vendetta against Garrow's attorneys? Even if they succeeded in disposing of Armani and Belge, they had to know that the court would appoint another attorney to defend Garrow.

Armani checked into the room he rented by the month at Zeiser's Inn. He called Belge's room, but his co-counsel was out. Rather than try to track Belge down, Armani decided to wait until morning to talk with him about what Latich had told him. Instead, he took advantage of the night to work until 2:00 A.M., carefully poring over the list of prosecution witnesses due to begin testifying the following day.

After a fitful, nightmare-riddled sleep, Armani pulled himself out of bed at 7:00 A.M. He showered, dressed, and walked downstairs to the dining room, where he took his customary table next to the large bay window overlooking the back garden. The waitress walked directly over and filled his coffee cup.

"Two eggs, basted, Canadian bacon, and whole wheat toast," Armani ordered. It was the same breakfast he ate every weekday morning at Zeiser's.

The waitress left without writing down his order. Armani sipped his coffee, glanced out the window, and noted that it was raining. He absent-mindedly reached for the linen napkin. As he unfolded it to lay it across his lap, he paused. There was a message printed in ballpoint pen across the napkin:

WE CAN TAKE YOU OUT AT ANY TIME. THAT KID KILLER BETTER NOT GET OFF.

Armani felt his stomach clench. Beads of perspiration blossomed on his upper lip. He quickly glanced around to see if anyone was watching him, but he was alone in the dining room. He stuffed the napkin into his jacket pocket and stood. When the waitress reappeared, carrying his breakfast on a tray, Armani asked, "Who was at this table before me?"

"Why, no one, Mr. Armani," she answered, unsure of what to do with the tray of food. "You're the first one in the dining room this morning."

Armani grabbed his briefcase and stalked out of the dining room. He left Zeiser's, jumped into his car, and sped off. About a mile and a half out of town, toward Wells, he pulled into the parking lot of the Blue Star Motel. It had quit raining. Armani marched up to the door marked *6* and knocked. Henry McCabe answered the door. The BCI investigator was dressed in suit pants and a T-shirt and held a plastic cup full of coffee.

Noting the lawyer's fearful, angry look, McCabe asked, "What's up, Frank?"

"Do you know what *this* is all about?" Armani demanded, handing McCabe the napkin.

McCabe read the printed message, then motioned Armani into his room.

"I heard a wild story last night from a friend of mine," Armani explained. "He said that some nuts from the Albany area were trying to buy a contract on Belge's and my life. I thought it was horse shit. Now, I'm not so sure."

"Mind if I keep this?" McCabe asked.

"I'm done eating," Armani said.

"We heard about it last week," McCabe said. "We can't find out exactly who's behind it, but your friend's information is right on the money."

"Kill Belge and me because we're defending Garrow?"

"Of course there's no logic behind it, Frank. There are a lot of strange people walking around out there."

"So what the hell do I do, for cryin' out loud. You're telling me that I have to try this case with some lunatic hit man stalking me?"

"Chances are it's just a bluff—to try and get you to slack off a little on Garrow's defense. You know, not try so hard," McCabe suggested.

"*Chances are* it's a bluff! What do I have to do, get myself killed to find out it's not?"

"Since we heard about those people trying to buy the hit, I've had a member of our assassination unit watching you for your protection," McCabe explained.

"Great," Armani said sarcastically, shaking his head.

"In view of this threat to you this morning, I'll want to issue a detail of men to stay with you and Belge at all times—something visible to scare these people off from attempting anything."

"I can't believe this," Armani let out a long breath. "Your men going to sleep in my room with me?"

"Naw." McCabe laughed. "They'll just sit outside your door at night. And, based on Belge's track record with the ladies, my men will probably bid for the detail to watch him."

"Very funny," Armani said. "How the hell am I supposed to do my work with a bunch of cops under my feet? How do I interview Garrow if there's a cop in the room?"

"We'll work that out."

"I don't know, Henry. Maybe I'd just as soon look out after myself."

"Don't fool around with this thing, Frank. These people could mean business. This is serious stuff."

"Yeah, okay," Armani said. He stepped toward the door. "I'll let you know about the police protection later. Right now I need to get down to the courthouse."

"Just watch yourself," McCabe said, walking out of the room with Armani. He waited in the parking lot while the lawyer drove away.

Armani ran into Belge outside the courthouse. Belge was playing on the front lawn with his hunting dog, a Chesapeake retriever named Chardon.

"Watch this," Belge called when he spotted Armani walking toward him. He removed one of his black alligator loafers and tossed it halfway across the wet grass. The white-and-gold-dappled dog bounded across the lawn and wrapped his jaws around the shoe. He brought it back and dropped it at Belge's feet.

"Not even a toothmark on it," Belge said, as he examined his loafer. "A helluva animal; he can retrieve anything. Maybe we can get him on the payroll as a private investigator on this case?"

"Only if he can shoot straight," Armani answered.

Belge wheeled around to face the other lawyer. "What the hell's that supposed to mean?"

Armani told him about his conversation with Matt Latich, the napkin on his table in Zeiser's dining room, and what Henry McCabe had just told him in the motel room.

"No dice on the police protection," Belge stated emphatically.

"Why not? You think I'm going to feel exactly relaxed

knowing I'm working in the crosshairs of some maniac's gun?"

"And I say that this entire thing was probably cooked up by the authorities," Belge said. "They want a conviction so bad, I wouldn't put it past them to come up with some bogus Mafia-type death threat like this in order to get someone into our room to eavesdrop on us."

"That's a little far-fetched, isn't it?"

"Nothing would surprise me about this case. Didn't the BCI tail us while we were searching for the bodies? And haven't we both suspected that our office and home phones have been tapped?"

"You have a point. But how would Matt Latich find out about the hit contract if there wasn't some truth to it?"

"Look, Frank," Belge said. "Don't you think the BCI knows that you stop at that same restaurant every Sunday night to feed your face? Would it be so hard for them to have a couple of their boys stop in there in order to plant the information with Latich about the hit contract? As far as the napkin with the love note written on it, you eat breakfast at the same table in the same restaurant every morning. You've got the spontaneity of an oak dresser. You're such an easy setup for something like this, it isn't funny."

Armani thought Belge's explanation made some sense.

"So what do we do?" Armani asked.

"Arm ourselves and change hotels every night," Belge answered, reaching down to pet his dog.

"This thing is unbelievable," Armani said. He looked skyward and tried rubbing some of the tension from the back of his neck.

"Nobody said this case would come off by the book." Belge threw his shoe once again for his dog to retrieve.

21

June 13–17, 1974

As THE TRIAL got under way, Armani and Belge began carrying handguns in their briefcases. They kept loaded shotguns in the trunk of Armani's car and hired a private investigator, John Orloff, as their bodyguard. Orloff was a retired Troy, New York, policeman.

To ensure they didn't establish a predictable pattern in their sleeping arrangements, the two lawyers rotated each night between several motels within a ten-mile radius of the Lake Pleasant courthouse. In addition, each week they shuffled the list of motels to alter the sequence of their lodging. As for their field office, located in a room they had rented for that purpose at Zeiser's, they weren't as flexible. The sheer volume of paperwork and mass of books and other court-related material precluded them from constantly shifting the location of their office. They were forced into a set pattern that made them easier targets for an assassin's bullet.

The anxiety and precautions resulting from the death threat, together with their debilitating court schedule and late nights going over the daily court transcripts and preparing for the next day's session, quickly exhausted Belge and Armani.

Added to this was the reception they were given by the local townspeople, people convinced that Garrow was guilty and that Belge and Armani, simply by virture of their defending the murder suspect, should be on trial with Garrow. Each day on the street, the defense attorneys were subjected to verbal abuse, cold shoulders, and physical threats. These came not only from locals, but also from the curious who had traveled some distance to Lake Pleasant in hopes of being admitted to the courtroom. There were middle-of-the-night hate calls, phone calls that reached them despite their tactic of changing motels each night. Armani's car was vandalized on several occasions, and one night while relaxing after court in a Speculator bar, the two attorneys were forced to fight their way out of the place.

This hostility was not directed exclusively at Belge and Armani. John Zeiser, owner of the inn in which the two lawyers maintained their office and took many of their meals, was continually harassed. His business suffered, and he had to endure slurs and rejection from people he had known for twenty years.

This attitude of hate carried inside the jail. Late one night, the deputy sheriff assigned to guard Garrow walked by Garrow's cell, tossed the defendant a clothespin, and said, "Here, you lousy kid-raper, clip off your balls with this."

An enraged and despondent Garrow pulled the spring wire loose from the clothespin and punctured a hole in the artery of his right arm with it. He wasn't discovered until the following morning, but despite losing a great deal of blood, Garrow survived his suicide attempt.

There were a few bright moments during the opening weeks of the trial. These took place mostly at Zeiser's Bar, where much of the steam of the daily courtroom tensions were let off. A couple of evenings each week, Armani and Belge were joined at Zeiser's Bar by Norman Mordue, William Intemann, Judge George Marthen, and Henry McCabe. With several drinks under their belts, the six of them took to arguing some point of the day's trial proceedings until Judge Marthen ruled that the discussion had gone too far and banged his shoe on the bar. Several reporters were always present during these heated discussions. By agreement, Zeiser's was off limits as a news source. None of what was argued at the bar appeared in the media; what was said there stayed there. Any reporter who violated that agreement found himself banished from Zeiser's and from the courtroom for the duration of the trial.

Francis Belge was the unquestioned star of these after-court gatherings at Zeiser's. One time Belge stalked into the taproom and announced that there would be a major leak in the Garrow case the following day. The next morning, at the preordained time and location, Belge greeted the group of alerted, anxious reporters and produced the major "leak" in the case: a bunch of wild leeks he had picked in the woods.

Belge's antics seemed to be his way of testing the limits of the New York State statute that guaranteed an attorney immunity from prosecution during a trial in which he was participating. It was a law that dated back to the time when a lawyer who represented an unpopular issue or person tended to find himself locked up on some trumped-up charge. It was behind this law that Belge continually ducked during the Garrow trial to shield himself from prosecution for a seemingly unending string of provocative gestures—like driving through the restful town to court at seven o'clock every morning in a truck badly in need of a muffler grinning and waving at the local cops, who were powerless to move against him.

Armani was initially annoyed at Belge's behavior outside the courtroom. Then he caught on to why his co-counsel was working so hard at becoming more of a celebrity than Robert Garrow. Belge meant to provide some comic relief from the grisly drama unfolding within the walls of the Hamilton County courthouse. By thumbing his nose at them with his antics, the fiercely independent Belge was paradoxically endearing himself to the fiercely independent inhabitants of the Adirondack region. In being cast in the role of a lovable rogue, Belge was scoring points with the locals. He was counting on the resultant friendly attitude to reverse some of the animosity Hamilton County residents had directed toward him and Armani. Belge hoped this improved attitude might somehow filter into the courtroom and influence the jury. After all, you can't loathe someone you find amusing.

By way of contrast, Belge was all business in the courtroom. It was as though, at nine o'clock each morning, Belge metamorphosed from jester into the brilliant, wily trial attorney that he truly was. With Armani providing the backup research, Belge aggressively cross-examined each of the thirty-three prosecution witnesses. With each one, he skillfully worked to establish that Garrow was insane under the New York State law that stated: "A person is not criminally liable for conduct, if at the time of such conduct, as a result of mental disease or defect, he lacks substantial capacity to know or appreciate the nature and consequences of such conduct or that such conduct was wrong."

The most damaging prosecution testimony against Garrow came from Nick Fiorello, Daniel Freeman, and Carol Ann Freeman (she had married Daniel Freeman earlier that year). The three young people described Garrow's demeanor as cool and calculating the morning he slipped into their campground and killed Philip Domblewski. They testified that the defendant seemed to know exactly what he was doing and was completely under his own control. Carol Ann Freeman spoke of how Garrow had treated her politely, how he was concerned that the rope didn't hurt her wrists as he tied her to the tree. In all, the testimony of the three young people severely discredited the defense's contention that Garrow was deranged and in a frenzied, hallucinatory state that morning.

Further damaging testimony came from Dr. Jack Davies, a New York State pathologist from Albany. Davies stated that the five wounds in Domblewski's chest had been inflicted slowly and deliberately—they weren't the act of a man operating in an insane rage. The courtroom was further shocked when Davies testified that four of the five stab wounds weren't of a fatal nature. They had been meant to torture the victim.

The rest of the prosecution's witnesses created a web of evidence that tied Garrow to the crime. In his cross-examination, other than attempting to encourage the idea that Garrow was out of his mind and didn't understand the nature or consequences of his act, Belge made only small efforts to discredit the testimony of the prosecution's witnesses. He had already admitted that his client had killed Philip Domblewski. Rather, Belge chose repeatedly to interrupt Intemann or Mordue, in particular to assert that the post-mortem photographs of Domblewski, along with Carol Ann Freeman's graphic descriptions of the murder scene, were meant only to inflame the jury.

On June 17th, with the prosecution having completed its case, it was time for the defense to begin calling its witnesses. It was thundering and raining outdoors when George Marthen brought the court into session. The fifty or so people seated on the hard benches, the majority of them radio, television, and newspaper reporters, had waited in line outside the courthouse since six that morning for the opportunity to observe the day's proceedings. Most of the spectators were already perspiring, and many used makeshift fans for relief from the courtroom's stiflingly hot and humid air.

Armani and Belge sat waiting at the defense table. Belge was writing something on the back of the previous day's court transcripts, while Armani busily arranged his notes so they were in the order in which the defense witnesses were to appear. He felt satisfied with the psychiatrists he had subpoenaed; he had done his homework well. The psychiatrists who were to begin appearing today had examined Garrow thoroughly. Each would testify that Robert Garrow was a schizophrenic who suffered from a thought disorder so severe that he could not have appreciated the nature or consequences of his conduct the morning he had killed Philip Domblewski. What's more, Armani believed that the jury would consider the psychiatrists' testimony beyond reproach. They were all top men in their field.

Seated in his wheelchair next to Armani and Belge and chatting amiably with the two deputy sheriffs assigned to guard him was Robert Garrow. Dressed in the black suit Armani had purchased for him, Garrow appeared gaunt. His glasses looked too large for his ashen face. His left arm was held in a sling inside his white shirt. His left foot, in which he had sustained his most serious gunshot wounds, was still in a cast, propped out straight by the wheelchair stanchion.

At the prosecutor's table, to the left of the defense counsel's table and across the courtroom, sat William Intemann and Norman Mordue. Up to this point in the trial, the Onondaga County assistant district attorney had handled the major portion of the people's case.

"Is the defense ready?" Judge Marthen asked, glancing down at Armani and Belge.

"The defense is ready, your honor," Belge answered. He felt suffocated in his navy blue summer suit and starched white shirt.

The judge nodded, then, looking down at Intemann and Mordue, asked, "The prosecution ready to proceed?"

"The prosecution is ready, your honor," Intemann answered.

As Belge moved to the front of the courtroom to launch the

defense case, Armani found himself gripped by the familiar anxious feeling in his stomach, the twinge of apprehension that had visited him many times during the trial. His anxiety came in part from fatigue. Armani had spent most of the preceding week chasing around New York State subpoenaing witnesses to testify on Garrow's behalf. He was also nervous because, beginning today, the prosecution would be testing the result of *his* research, questioning his interviews with witnesses and the overall psychiatric basis for Garrow's "innocent by reason of insanity" plea.

"You may call your first witness, Mr. Belge," Judge Marthen said.

"The defense calls Robert Garrow," Belge announced.

Garrow's head jerked up, and his hand flew away from where it was shielding his eyes. His face was full of question, and his mouth hung open.

"What the . . .?" Armani blurted.

"*Robert Garrow* as your opening witness?" Judge Marthen, too, showed his surprise.

A loud buzz of conversation drifted up from the spectator gallery. News reporters scribbled busily on notepads.

"That's correct, your honor," Belge repeated. "Robert Garrow will testify on his own behalf."

"We need a conference, your honor," Armani called. He jumped to his feet, all the time glaring at Belge. "The defense asks for a recess."

"The court grants the defense a ten-minute recess," Marthen ordered. "Everyone will remain seated while the sheriff escorts the jury from the courtroom."

"One more thing, your honor," Belge requested. "We would like to use the safe room downstairs, and we would like Mr. Garrow to join Mr. Armani and me."

"Permission granted on both requests," Marthen declared. "Will the sheriff's deputy accompany the defendant downstairs to the room off the kitchen."

Within moments Armani, Belge, and a glowering, morose Robert Garrow were gathered in the storeroom off the kitchen. The windowless cubicle had been designed as a safe room in which the defense could hold conferences without fear of being interrupted or overheard.

"Will you please tell me what the hell this is all about?" Armani demanded. "Especially after I spent a week busting my gut to subpoena witnesses to testify that Garrow was a model father, husband, and worker who seemed incapable of committing the crime for which he's been charged—so that the psychiatrists can show how he's two different people."

"Garrow testifies first. It's our only chance," Belge explained. "We have to shock the jury into seeing that he is insane, and his testimony will lay in the foundation for the psychiatrists' reports and all that other stuff you've got."

"I don't know about this," Garrow sounded. "I'm not sure I *want* to testify."

"You've got to trust me, Bob," Belge implored, looking down at the defendant.

"What are you going to ask him?" Armani demanded. "We haven't had the chance to coach him in his testimony."

"It's better that he hasn't been coached," Belge countered.

"He could sink his own case."

"He'll do fine. The more spontaneous his responses, the better it'll look to the jury. We want him to appear as close to the *exact* kind of person that he is as possible."

"I'd like to know what you're going to ask me about up there," Garrow requested.

"Just go along with me on this, Bob. Please," Belge implored. "I know what I'm doing."

A stunned Armani stood staring at Belge. Once again Belge had made a major decision in the case without consulting him. Armani knew that if this eleventh-hour ploy of bringing Garrow on the witness stand backfired, there would be no way to turn things around. Even the psychiatrists' testimony couldn't undo Garrow's testimony if the defendant severely damaged his own case from the witness stand. Belge's was a do-or-die move. And yet, Armani had no real basis from which to challenge Belge's tactic. Up to this point his co-counsel had done an excellent job of interjecting the continuous thread of Garrow's insanity throughout the prosecution witnesses' testimony. Belge had subtly but effectively accomplished his goal of leaving just enough question in the jurors' minds to allow him to prove Garrow's mental instability when the defense's expert witnesses took the stand.

"What do you say, Bob?" Belge asked. "Are you going to trust me?"

Garrow stared hard at Belge.

"You have to believe me when I say it's our only chance to get you an insanity verdict," Belge continued.

"Okay. We'll do it your way," Garrow assented. "But I'm warning you. If this thing blows up, I'm getting out of here. I've already got a plan. . . ."

"You what?" Armani blurted.

"I'm gonna tie up the priest who's been visiting me every night, take his clothes, and make it into those woods behind the courthouse."

"Make it into the woods!" Armani said incredulously. "You can't even walk, for cryin' out loud."

"Don't worry about that," Garrow answered, confidently enough that his attorneys wondered if perhaps he could actually pull it off.

"And I'm telling you, Bob," Belge informed, "that you won't make it fifty feet. I have it on good source that the BCI has a sniper team operating under orders to gun you down if you try to run. The cops are scared to death that if you get away, they'll never catch you again. You got those bastards so freaked out, they practically think you can walk through those jailhouse walls."

Garrow smiled. The fact that the BCI held him in such high esteem amused him.

"All right," Belge said, checking his watch. "It's time to get upstairs."

"This had better work, Belge," Garrow said ominously before turning his wheelchair to face the door.

The look Armani tossed Belge seconded the defendant's sentiments.

The courtroom was alive with conversation when Belge and Armani walked back down the aisle to the defense table. Garrow, his wheelchair guided by a deputy sheriff, followed them to the table.

Everyone fell silent when Judge Marthen stepped out of his chambers and, with a rustle of his robes, took his seat. Ascertaining that the jury was in place, Marthen declared, "Court is back in session. The prosecution ready?"

"We're ready, your honor," a perplexed-looking Norman Mordue answered.

"The defense ready?"

"The defense is ready, judge," Belge responded.

Garrow was wheeled to a spot in front of the witness stand. While the defendant was sworn in, Armani angrily stuffed copies of the psychiatrists' reports into his briefcase. As was everyone else in the room, including Garrow, Armani was waiting for Belge to play his hand.

Looking confident, Belge walked around the defense table and stopped at a place just in front of Garrow. The defendant, shielding his eyes with his right hand, was staring at the floor.

"Start looking at me and the jury," Belge commanded with a stern edge to his voice.

Garrow obediently dropped his hand to his lap and looked up at his attorney.

Belge began the questioning by asking Garrow about his childhood. While answering, the defendant kept lowering his head. In his rambling responses, he continually referred to his brothers and sisters as "it" and "they." To Robert Garrow, his family members were objects rather than thinking, feeling human beings. Garrow revealed that his father was a drunk who had beat him regularly. He told how his mother would frequently fly into a rage and beat him savagely with a pinchbar, piece of stove wood, wide leather belt, or anything she could grab. He described how he had been sent away to live and work on a farm when he was seven years old. He testified that, during the summer and other school vacations, he had risen at three o'clock each morning to milk the cows and then worked all day until eleven o'clock at night, six days a week. During the school year, the schedule was the same, except that he was allowed to attend daytime classes.

"What did you do with those animals on that farm, Robert?" Belge asked, interrupting the defendant's rambling narrative of his life on the farm as a child.

Garrow lowered his head.

"Now, c'mon. Stop that!" Belge ordered. "Look at me, and tell me what you did with the animals."

"Objection," Mordue called. "He is badgering his own witness."

"Objection sustained—" Judge Marthen began.

"I realize the answer he wants, sir," Garrow interrupted. "But it's not a decent answer."

"You've been asked the question, Mr. Garrow," the judge ruled.

"All right, sir," Garrow responded. "I think the word they use today . . . with a woman you have intercourse. I used to have it with the animals. Put it that way."

A soft buzzing filled the courtroom as astonished and horrified spectators talked to one another.

"When did you start?" Belge asked.

"When I was probably about ten, eleven, twelve years old, because I had no friends and I never used to play . . . I couldn't play basketball; I didn't know no children or anything. Of course I had to fool around with calves, horses, cows, you know."

"Did you ever get caught having intercourse with the animals?"

"Once. Mr. Maholleck caught me with a cow."

"What happened?"

"Nothing. He waited until later and told me that it wasn't right to have sex with animals."

"Did Mr. Maholleck's warning stop you?"

"Naw. I kept doing it for ten years or so that I lived at Maholleck's—then after, on other farms I worked."

"What other trouble did you have on the Maholleck farm?" Belge pressed.

Garrow's eyes were cast downward, and he ran a hand nervously over his bald head.

"C'mon, Robert. Look at me and tell me."

"I used to put the milking machine on myself . . . you know, masturbate myself with it."

"When was the first time you ever kissed a girl?"

"On a train when I was in the service. I was about seventeen, I guess. I was going down to Florida. I was in the Air Force."

"How come you got out of the service early?"

"I got into trouble. I used to have dirty pictures and sell them; I stole a camera. I got a medical discharge after two years—it's on my parole record."

"How old were you when you first had intercourse with a woman?"

"When I got married . . . with my wife. I was twenty-three, I think. I'm not too good on dates and ages."

"When was the next time you got into trouble . . . after the service?" Belge asked.

"I was living in Albany with my sister, Florence. I busted up a Hot Shoppe where I worked when they wouldn't pay me what I had coming after I quit. I went to jail and got probation."

"You were assigned an attorney?"

"Yes, an attorney in Albany. He got me probation. Later I got picked up for violation, for not filling in the forms they sent me, and put back in jail."

"Tell us now what happened after the lawyer got you out of jail the second time," Belge directed.

"Objection," Mordue called out. "What does all of this have to do with the Domblewski murder?"

"I'm trying to have him tell us his life story, your honor," Belge explained. "It's relevant and connects to my line of defense."

"Objection overruled," Marthen said.

"My lawyer took me to his house to live—he lived with his mother. Then he got me a studio apartment and a job in a printing plant in Albany. You don't want me to go into the rest, do you?" an embarrassed, red-faced Garrow asked.

"Keep going. Tell us all that. Keep doing it."

"I got involved with a . . . the people refer today, like a fairy. He started up by taking pictures of me in his basement. A year goes by, and then it got down to where we got out in the woods. He had a time camera . . . used to take pictures and used to have me. . . ." Garrow explained, his voice trailing off.

"Used to have you what?"

"Have me play with him, et cetera, and so forth. He used to whip me with a leather thong."

"How long did this last?"

"For a few years, even after I got married."

"So while you were married, some sadist was whipping you. Did your wife ever find out?" Belge pressed.

"I think so. I had scars all over my back from the whip," Garrow answered, pointing with his good hand to his back.

"Did you get into trouble again in Albany?"

"I got arrested. I supposedly raped a girl and beat up her

boyfriend. At the time it happened, I didn't know it happened. I got mad at my wife that day at the house—I tore her dress. I was looking for the checkbook. She wouldn't let me have it, so I got mad at her and walked away from the house. . . . I got picked up by the detectives. They beat me up, pushed me down the stairs, dropped a typewriter on my foot because I would not sign the statement."

"You remember doing it, don't you?"

Garrow shook his head. "Only what the cops told me."

"Did you go to prison for that crime?"

"Dannemora, then I was transferred to Auburn. Eight years in all."

"In those eight years you were in jail, did you have any so-called sex with anybody?"

"Yes. I had a job in the galley. Me and the waterboy had what they refer to as sodomy."

"Oral or anal?"

"Both of them."

"After you got out of prison, where did you live?"

"In Syracuse."

"And something happened out of the ordinary in Syracuse, that right?" Belge asked.

Once again Garrow looked away from his attorney.

"C'mon, Robert. Tell me about it."

"I used to go away from my house at night or any time when I would get mad. Any time when I did something and my wife used to say I'm wrong, I used to get big headaches . . . the pressure would build," Garrow explained, indicating where by placing his hand on his forehead.

"What was the first unnatural act you did during this time?"

"I guess you'd call it rape," Garrow said nervously. Tears filled his eyes as he continued. "Listen, nobody knows about this. You're putting me on the spot here."

"I know it. What happened?"

Garrow began sobbing. Other than that, there wasn't a sound in the courtroom.

Armani jumped to his feet behind the defense table and shouted, "Your honor, Mr. Garrow has not been prepared to take the stand. I think I should have a chance to consult with him."

"Never mind, Mr. Armani," Belge shouted back.

"No, Frank, that's all right," Garrow said, trying to compose himself.

"Tell me about these rapes," Belge continued. "How many were there?"

"Seven, I think," Garrow answered, his voice breaking with emotion.

"You think?" Belge asked, amid audible gasps from the courtroom spectators.

"I never remembered doing any of them. I swear." Garrow removed his glasses and wiped his tears away with the sleeve of his suit jacket. "I would read the paper the next day and put the pieces together, and it would dawn on me that I had committed the rapes."

"Which paper?"

"The Syracuse paper. The rapes all took place in Syracuse—in parks."

"Tell us about them," Belge persisted.

"One was in Schiller Park, I think they call it, because I used to take my daughter swimming there. And this broad was in a car, she was naked with another guy on top of her, and I opened the door. Of course I used language telling them I was a park patrol or something and scared the guy off and took her in the park, and I had intercourse with her. I don't know her name; I don't know any of their names."

Belge turned slightly and glanced at the jury. The twelve men and women all had horrified, astonished looks on their faces.

"When was the next time you committed an immoral act?" Belge asked.

"I think it happened in the same park. About the same thing happened. The next time it happened in the cemetery, not too far from where I lived."

"Tell us how that happened."

"I think the cemetery is called Morningdale Cemetery. It was my day off. I couldn't sleep all that night; I just had to get out of my house. So after I got a few Excedrin and Alka-Seltzer, I left the house and went up to the cemetery. This girl was walking, and I supposedly had a gun, which was a cap gun, and we marched off in the bushes, and we had intercourse. I didn't remember it till the next day when I saw it in the papers and realized that the description fit me perfectly."

"There were others?"

"Yeah, there were others," Garrow answered. He had to pause to compose himself. "All the same way. I'd pretend I was a park patrol or a cop, then I'd have intercourse with them."

"When was the last time you committed a rape in Syracuse? Before you were captured in Witherbee, Robert?"

"It was after the car accident."

"What happened to you in the car accident?"

"Got smashed up. I was driving, and it was a policeman's son on the passenger side, and my boy was in back."

"You committed an immoral act after that accident?" Belge pressed.

"There was a couple of young girls that I got involved with somewhere out in the town of Geddes," Garrow answered. He looked at the floor.

"Robert, when you talked to me in the beginning, you were facing me. Do you mind doing that now?"

Garrow looked up at Belge. His eyes were red and his face tear-streaked. "I supposedly had sodomy with those two young girls. I guess one of them was around ten or eleven, according to the indictment."

"C'mon, Robert. You're telling me that you 'supposedly' had sodomy with those two young girls?" Belge probed. "You remember doing it, don't you?"

"Yeah, I mean I remember parts. I was able to piece it together later, when the cops picked me up and questioned me."

"So you're saying that you committed seven rapes in how long of a period of time?"

"I'm not too good on dates."

"C'mon, Robert," Belge pressed. "Now, look at me and answer the question."

Garrow's eyes shifted to Belge. He drew in a couple of deep breaths that sounded throughout the courtroom as sobs. "I committed the rapes over about a two-year period."

"Okay, Robert, I want you to tell us about your health over the two years before you were captured in Witherbee," Belge ordered. He felt satisfied that he was producing the reaction among the jury that he had hoped for. Garrow's testimony thus far had shocked them.

Garrow talked about the pressure that had built within him over the two years preceding his capture. His headaches had worsened and had come more regularly. He operated in the grip of a paranoia so severe that many nights he slept in his garage or in the woods directly behind his Berwyn Avenue residence, in order to escape if the police came to his house after him. The only thing that relieved the headaches and the paranoia was to commit another rape, as if the crime were a release. Then he would be granted a brief respite from the pressure, only to have it build up again in a few weeks or months.

On one occasion, when the pressure in his head had reached the bursting point, he left his home and drove to Mineville to visit his ailing father. He stopped en route in Wevertown for a roadside nap. Upon awakening, he noticed a white BMW parked in back of him. Piecing events together from his spotty recollection and responding to Belge's prodding, Garrow told how he had argued with Daniel Porter and then stabbed him to death. With everyone in the courtroom listening with a horrified intensity, Garrow told how he had abducted Susan Petz and repeatedly sexually abused her in the tent he had pitched on the hill above his parents' house. Then he'd stabbed her to death and dumped her body into the airshaft.

The questioning moved on to Alicia Hauck. At Belge's insistence, Garrow admitted that, after picking her up hitchhiking and raping her, he had killed the Hauck girl and hidden her body in Oakwood Cemetery.

Finally Garrow described how he had tied up Daniel and Carol Ann Freeman, Nick Fiorello, and Philip Domblewski. Talking freely about stabbing Domblewski to death, Garrow referred to the young man as 'it,' as he had some of his other victims, rather than by the personal pronoun form.

When queried by Belge as to why he had murdered Daniel Porter and Philip Domblewski, since it was apparent that he was after the girls they were with, Garrow testified that they had reminded him of the long-haired man he had found in bed with his girl friend when he was seventeen. When confronted by Porter and Domblewski, that old memory had appeared in his head, and some power within him had forced him to murder the two young men.

As his testimony wound down, Garrow covered his face with his good hand and wept openly. Everyone in the courtroom, including the judge and the prosecution lawyers, sat mute in disbelief. In addition to admitting to the murder for which he was being tried, Garrow had just confessed to having committed three other homicides and seven rapes.

At the completion of Garrow's seven hours on the witness stand, Judge Marthen adjourned court for the day. Once the clearly horrified and astonished jurors were led from the courtroom, the spectators filed mutely from the room. What everyone had heard in court that day exceeded anything they had expected to witness during this trial.

Armani and Belge were met on the front steps of the courthouse by the horde of reporters. A barrage of questions was fired at the two attorneys. Belge requested quiet by raising his right hand.

"Because the trial is still under way," he stated, "we will take no questions. We don't wish to prejudice our client's rights in any way. Mr. Armani and I will limit ourselves to making a joint statement to you about today's proceedings."

Flashbulbs ignited against the storm-darkened sky, and television cameras silently whirred. The news reporters waited with pads and pencils poised. Belge began.

"What you heard in the courtroom today, namely the defendant Robert Garrow's testimony that he murdered Susan Petz, Alicia Hauck, and Daniel Porter, has released Mr. Armani and me from a confidence we've been sworn to maintain for nearly a year. The startling information revealed by Mr. Garrow has been the basis for a special and terrible burden Mr. Armani and I have carried since last August, when the defendant told us of these crimes. Since that time we have known that Mr. Garrow murdered Alicia Hauck, Susan Petz, and Daniel Porter. And moreover, in order to ascertain the credibility of Mr. Garrow's confession to us, Mr. Armani and I located and viewed the bodies of Alicia Hauck and Susan Petz during the month of August of last year.

"We can't tell you how badly we wanted to pass on some hint about the fate of their daughters to the parents of Alicia Hauck and Susan Petz. But we were prevented from doing so by the Canon of Ethics we swore to uphold when we were admitted to the bar. Specifically, Canon Four, which dictates that no lawyer can breach the confidentiality of his client in any manner, that he must not violate the sacred trust that exists between himself and his client. Therefore, despite the unbelievable pressure from the press and from law-enforcement officials on us to do so, and in the face of the awful agony we felt from knowing the horror the Hauck and Petz families were undergoing, Mr. Armani and I were legally bound not to divulge that we had found the bodies of those two girls."

Finished with his statement, Belge pushed through the throng of stunned reporters. Behind him, with eyes cast downward, followed Frank Armani. The two attorneys ignored the wave of questions coming from behind them. As Armani and Belge reached the Mercedes, one reporter's voice carried above the others. "You guys are going to have a helluva battle on your hands over what you did."

Armani unlocked the car door and jumped into the front seat. He reached over, unlocked Belge's door, and started the car. He headed the Mercedes out of the courthouse parking lot. News photographers ran alongside the car, snapping off last-minute pictures. Armani stared silently ahead. As they rounded the turn and moved down the courthouse driveway, they noticed a line of BCI Swat team members stationed all along the edge of the woods across from the open field adjacent to the jail.

"So much for our bug-free safe room," Belge commented disgustedly. "You can bet your ass that they're going to have their eyes peeled for a priest going for a walk in those woods tonight."

The best Armani could do was to nod his head.

During the ten-minute drive to Fowler's Christian Camp on Lake Pleasant, where they were staying the night, Armani kept mulling over in his head the words the reporter had yelled as the two lawyers were making their way to the Mercedes: "You guys are going to have a helluva battle on your hands over what you did." Though he had no way of predicting the full extent of what might be coming, Armani realized the time was nearing when he and Belge would have to pay for upholding their client's right of confidentiality.

By the time Armani eased his car to a stop in front of Fowler's Christian Camp Lodge, his mind had seized on something else: the deep churning anger he felt over the way Belge had handled Garrow's defense.

Without saying a word to one another, the two men walked into the deserted, spacious parlor, stepped around clusters of red leather and maple furniture, and headed for the staircase.

"You want a drink?" Belge asked as they hit the second floor landing.

"Sure," Armani answered, having to force out his reply.

Once they were in his room, Armani grabbed the bottle of Chivas Regal from the top of the dresser.

"I'll get some ice," Belge said, disappearing out the door.

Armani's hand shook as he poured the two drinks. The fury he felt forced him to look away when his co-counsel returned to the room carrying a bucketful of ice.

"A little rain for the fire," Belge announced. He loaded a handful of ice into each drink.

Belge's nonchalant, glib manner set Armani off. His craggy face contorted, and he exploded in anger. "I gotta tell you, you bastard, that I totally disagree with what you did in that courtroom, today. Bringing Garrow on the stand as our opening witness was a dumb move. It inflamed the jury and sunk the case for us."

"Guess time will tell, won't it, Frank?" Belge answered. He toasted Armani with his drink.

"I'm also mad as hell at you for not first consulting with me about what you wanted to do—especially after I broke my butt getting witnesses here today from all over New York State to testify."

"What can I tell you? I only made up my mind to put Garrow on the stand on my way to court this morning."

"That's your problem, Belge. That's why you can't get along with anyone. You only think about yourself, about what's best for you, and don't give a damn about what anyone else thinks or feels."

Drinking deeply of his scotch, Belge watched Armani over the rim of his glass.

"I'm probably the best friend you have in the world, and still you run over me, like you did today."

Belge's lips twisted into a sarcastic smile. He set his drink down on the dresser.

"The way I see it, Belge," Armani challenged, "Garrow ain't the only nut in that courtroom."

"Up yours, Armani."

Armani dropped his glass on the dresser. The scotch splashed onto the top of the oak surface. Removing his eyeglasses, he said, "I've had it with all your crap."

For a few seconds, the two men stood toe-to-toe as if frozen in place by one another's furious stare. Belge made the first move. He reached out and shoved Armani. Armani retaliated with a roundhouse right that caught Belge flush on the forehead, producing a sound like a baseball thrown against a concrete wall. A stupid, amused look on his face, Belge answered the punch with a right lead of his own that split Armani's upper lip open.

Releasing all of the emotion and tension stored up from their weeks in the Lake Pleasant courthouse, Belge and Armani began swinging wildly at one another. Belge was getting the worst of it. He grabbed Armani from behind in a bearhug and tried wrestling him to the floor. But the shorter man was too strong and too determined to be taken down. Instead, Armani leaned forward, lifted Belge off his feet, and carried him around the room piggyback style. He broke the taller lawyer's grip by falling backwards against the dresser, sending Belge, along with the bottle of scotch and bucket of ice, crashing to the floor. Belge scurried to his feet and came at Armani like a windmill. Throughout the scuffle, neither man uttered a word. There was only the labored, grunting breathing of two out-of-shape men.

Armani ended it. He sank a chopping powerful right into Belge's midsection, then straightened the taller lawyer up with a right uppercut that transformed his nose into something resembling a mashed tomato.

A sweating, wheezing Armani was standing over the unconscious Belge when someone knocked at the door.

"Everything all right in there?" It was Reverend Chisum, director of Fowler's Christian Camp.

Armani walked to the door, opened it, and let himself out of the room.

"Any trouble, Frank?" Reverend Chisum asked. The gray-haired minister's face wore an expression of concern and fear.

"No problem. Belge was a little tired from our long day in court, so he's lying down for a nap," Armani explained as he headed down the hall. "I'm going out to get something to eat. See you later, Reverend."

"That was some show in the courtroom today," Chisum called after him. He had been a regular spectator since the opening day of the trial.

"Yeah, some show." Armani rubbed his right hand as he walked down the stairs. He hoped he hadn't broken it.

A few minutes after midnight, a disheveled Frank Armani was seated at the oak writing table in Fowler's front parlor. He was alone in the room, and the only light was the triangle of gold cast by the desk lamp. Pen in hand, Armani was staring at the single sheet of white stationery positioned in the center of the desk. Strewn about the floor around his chair were several crumpled-up papers, letters Armani had begun but had discarded as being somehow inadequate to the task. He leaned forward and once again attempted to form his sentiments into words on the single sheet of Fowler Camp stationery:

Dear Mr. and Mrs. Petz:

I wish I could express to you how terribly I feel about the death of your daughter, Susan. I have daughters of my own, yet still can only imagine how profound your grief must be over Susan's loss. From everything I've been able to learn, she was an extremely decent and good girl, one to whom the cruel and unjust hand of destiny dealt such a horrible fate.

I don't know, Mr. Petz, if you can find it in your heart to forgive me for lying to you in my office the day you came to inquire about your daughter. I can only ask that you understand my position at the time. . . .

Armani lifted the pen from the paper, then wiped his shirtsleeve across his face to blot away the tears. He reached across the desk for his drink. Sipping the scotch, he read what he had written. Unsatisfied, he angrily grabbed the sheet of paper and wadded it. He tossed it to the floor and took another swallow of scotch.

Placing the glass on the desk, Frank Armani crossed his palms on the oak surface, slowly lowered his forehead until it rested on his bruised hands, and began sobbing.

"Damn, damn, damn it all," he mumbled, the words choked by the painful emotions that ravaged him.

22

Third Week of June 1974

THE FOLLOWING DAY Robert Garrow was cross-examined by
the prosecution. Norman Mordue worked hard to shake Garrow's earlier testimony about not remembering the particulars
of the Domblewski killing, about being in a hallucinatory,
blacked-out state when he had committed the murder. Several
times throughout the morning session, Garrow exploded with
anger, but he held to his story.

During the afternoon recess, an unexpected visitor appeared
in the courtroom. Onondaga County District Attorney Jon
Holcombe approached the defense table, where Frank Armani
and Francis Belge were preparing for the balance of the day's
session. Armani looked up from the stack of papers on the table
to the balding, tall, husky Holcombe. "Jon, what are you doing
here?"

Belge, his nose bandaged, glanced up but said nothing.
There was little love lost between him and Holcombe.

Holcombe moved a step closer, so that he was looking down
at the two attorneys. Behind him, the jury was being brought
back from recess. Judge George Marthen had just stepped out
of the door behind the bench.

"I'm here to inform you both that I feel you acted unethically and illegally by withholding information about the Petz
and Hauck murders," Holcombe said, loudly enough so his
voice carried to the jury box and to the judge's bench. "Since

the Hauck girl was murdered in Onondaga County, I've ordered the Syracuse police chief and my office to begin an investigation to ascertain if criminal charges can be brought against you."

Belge sat dumbfounded. Armani shook his head. He couldn't believe that Holcombe would make a public allegation of that nature, especially in a court of law. Something caused Armani to glance towards the judge's bench. George Marthen's face was crimson.

"Bailiff," Marthen ordered, "bring that man into my chambers—now!"

Judge Marthen did an about-face and rushed back into his chambers. Undersheriff Parker stepped alongside Jon Holcombe and escorted the Onondaga County district attorney into Marthen's chambers.

"What the hell are *you* doing in my courtroom?" Marthen demanded.

"I'm here on Onondaga County business—" Holcombe began.

"This is Hamilton County. You have no jurisdiction here," Marthen shot back. "I've broken my neck to make certain that this trial goes in right, and you show up and make some stupid comment like that to Armani and Belge."

"I released a press statement this morning about the improprieties committed by the two defense attorneys in this case." A slight smile creased Holcombe's thick lips. "I only stated to Belge and Armani what is already in the papers."

"I don't give a damn what the newspapers say," Marthen challenged. "We've had this jury sequestered since the opening of the trial, so they wouldn't be prejudiced by the media. We've already had to poll them twice, after they'd been subjected to minor press leaks. And you walk into my courtroom and shoot your mouth off in front of them about what's in the newspapers. Don't you realize that you've set us up for a possible mistrial? Not to mention what Garrow can do because of your threat to his attorneys? All he has to do is cry that you've prevented Belge and Armani from doing their jobs, and thus he's been denied due process. The Appellate Court would reverse a conviction any day on that one."

"I only warned the two attorneys about a fact of law—"

"Get the hell out of here, Holcombe!" Marthen interrupted,

shaking with fury. "Get the hell out of my courtroom, and get the hell out of Hamilton County. I'm warning you, if you're not across the county line in a half an hour, I'm going to have the sheriff pick you up for obstructing justice."

The smile drained from Holcombe's face. His right eye began twitching.

"You haven't heard the last of this, judge—"

"Get out!" Marthen yelled. "I've got a trial to run, and I'm not going to let you screw it up. You've got a half an hour to be out of this county."

Holcombe started for the door leading to the courtroom.

"No," Marthen barked, pointing the other way. "Out *that* door! It leads to the parking lot. I don't want you to even be *seen* by anyone in that courtroom."

As Holcombe let himself out the door, Marthen turned to Undersheriff Parker, who was standing off to one side and had witnessed the scene. "I want you to put out a call on the radio. If Holcombe's not out of Hamilton County in thirty minutes, have him picked up. If you do, I have a good mind to let him share a cell with Garrow."

That same afternoon, Mary Armani drove up to Lake Pleasant with her two daughters. She and her daughters planned to attend the afternoon court session, then spend an Adirondack summer weekend with Frank. That would allow a little relaxation while Armani prepared for Monday's court session.

They arrived at the crowded courtroom a little after three o'clock. Armani had arranged reserved seats for them behind the defense table. It was the first time Mary, Debbie, and Dorina had been inside the Lake Pleasant courtroom, and they were excited at the prospect of viewing firsthand the proceedings that were gathering so much publicity. Since getting under way, the Garrow trial had been regular feature news in the Syracuse media. Now, after two defense attorneys had revealed secret knowledge of the whereabouts of the Petz and Hauck bodies, Armani's name had been splashed across the headlines of almost every major newspaper in the eastern United States. This was also the first time Debbie and Dorina had ever seen their father in action in a courtroom.

Mary, Debbie, and Dorina took their seats just as Norman Mordue was completing his cross-examination of Robert Garrow. Under the pressure of Mordue's penetrating and relentless attempt to discredit Garrow's insanity claim, the defendant had alternated between bitter hostility and an open show of sorrow.

"I have no further questions for the defendant," Mordue announced to Judge Marthen.

There followed a moment of silence in the courtroom. Garrow, his hand covering his downcast eyes, sobbed audibly in his wheelchair in front of the witness stand.

Judge Marthen glanced down at Belge and asked, "You have any further questions for your witness?"

"None, your honor," Belge answered.

"The witness is excused."

The portly, red-faced, and gray-haired Undersheriff Parker walked to the front of the courtroom and wheeled Garrow to his spot at the end of the defense table, next to Armani. For the next few seconds, while Belge riffled through the stack of papers that were his notes, Garrow sat hunch-shouldered, shielding his face with his good hand and staring down at his lap.

"We'd like a brief recess, your honor," Belge stated, seemingly unable to locate the piece of paper for which he was hunting.

"Court grants a ten-minute recess," Marthen said. "Everyone remain seated until the jury is taken from the courtroom."

As the jury filed out of the box, Armani turned to his family.

"How's it going?" Mary asked, reaching out to touch his arm.

"Anybody's guess at this point," the attorney said quietly.

Mary turned her eyes to Belge, smiled politely, and asked, "How are you, Francis?"

"I'll make it."

"What happened to your nose?" Mary asked, noting the bandages over the bridge of his nose.

"Punched a guy in the fist with it." Belge smiled. He shifted in his chair until he was facing Debbie and Dorina. "You girls are getting more beautiful every time I see you."

Dorina and Debbie each offered embarrassed smiles.

Mary Armani continued to chat with her husband and with Belge. Dorina, her hair tied into a pony tail, and dressed in a white summer blouse and blue skirt, let her glance move carefully to where Robert Garrow was seated in his wheelchair. As if feeling the young girl's eyes on his back, Garrow dropped his hand from his face and turned toward her. Their eyes locked for a moment, Garrow's hard, penetrating stare frightening Dorina. His lips turned upward in a smile. "Nice to see you again, Dorina."

The young woman's face froze in horror. She had to force herself to look away from Garrow's hypnotic stare. When she did, Dorina found herself looking into her sister's eyes.

"I didn't realize you knew Garrow," Debbie said softly.

"I *don't* know him," Dorina answered.

Debbie's eyes widened. There was only one way Garrow could have known who Dorina was. He had to have been stalking her. The idea that her sister might have been marked by Garrow as a rape victim or worse horrified Debbie.

Dorina suddenly bolted from her chair and headed out of the courtroom.

Mary Armani turned from her conversation with her husband and Belge and asked, "Where is she going?"

"She must need some air," Debbie answered, standing up. "I'll go outside with her."

"Don't be long," Frank Armani warned. "We'll be starting soon."

Frank and Mary Armani watched their oldest daughter walk down the center aisle, to the courtroom's double entrance doors. Robert Garrow watched, too.

After the weekend recess, the defense and prosecution took turns parading a battery of prominent psychiatrists and psychologists to the witness stand.

For their part, the defense relied heavily on doctors Franklin Reed and Jerry Morrow, both psychiatrists at Upstate Medical Center in Syracuse. Each corroborated the other's analysis of the defendant by citing an incident that occurred when Garrow was six years old. Garrow had been beaten half to death by his father for knocking down a few cornstalks while playing in the cornfield. This incident, the psychiatrists testified, severely traumatized Garrow. The boy realized that his father wouldn't have punished a cow that harshly for knocking down a few cornstalks and so began feeling himself worth less than an animal. Considering himself thusly, the psychiatrists stated, Garrow began viewing the world from an unthinking, unfeeling standpoint. He no longer considered people to be people. Instead, he saw them as he saw himself, as unfeeling objects who were less than animals in the importance of things and who were subject to abuse by others. That Garrow considered people this way, according to the psychiatrists, led to the defendant's sexual dysfunction, beginning with his having intercourse with animals. Reed and Morrow also stated that Garrow suffered from schizophrenia and couldn't have appreciated the nature and consequences of his act of killing Philip Domblewski. In essence, Garrow had seen Domblewski as an object and not a person, as something threatening to be removed from his path. Garrow, the psychiatrists testified, simply didn't know right from wrong.

Further, they stated, Garrow believed himself to be at the mercy of strange magnetic forces. He was powerless against these forces, his actions were totally dictated by their inner pull, and he went wherever they took him.

Dr. Morrow startled and mesmerized the courtroom when he revealed that, during one of his interviews with the defendant, he had induced Garrow to recreate the mental state he was experiencing at the time he killed Philip Domblewski.

"What did you say to him to get him to recreate this experience?" Belge asked Dr. Morrow.

"I asked him to close his eyes and imagine that I was a serious threat to him," the thin psychiatrist answered, nervously fingering his dark-rimmed glasses.

"He was able to do that?"

"At first he refused, saying that he had nothing against me. He didn't want to do it."

"But you kept after him to do so?"

"Yes." Morrow removed his glasses and wiped his brow with his handkerchief. "Mr. Garrow put his head down on the table and, in as moment, looked up at me."

"And what did you see?"

"It was a terrifying scene. I was stationed in Vietnam during the war, doing psychiatric work with soldiers suffering from battle-induced psychotic breaks, and nothing I saw over there frightened me as much as the look Garrow gave me—"

"Please, your honor," prosecuting attorney Mordue called. "I object. The witness is not answering the question."

"Objection overruled," Judge Marthen declared, himself deeply fascinated by the psychiatrist's testimony.

Morrow continued. "Mr. Garrow's pupils were enlarged, his face was beet red, and his neck seemed swollen to twice its size. His hands were opening and closing like he was in great pain or suffering with tremendous fury."

"Did he say anything to you at this time?" Belge prodded.

"Yes. Mr. Garrow mentioned that he was hearing a loud rushing in his ears, the sound of wind, and that his head pained him greatly. Then he referred to me as his father and said, 'I've got to kill it, Dad. I've got to kill you.' He started coming out of his chair toward me. I was absolutely paralyzed with fear. Then he snapped out of it and said, 'Don't be afraid. You're not my father. I won't hurt you.' "

"For what reason did you induce the defendant into this state?" Belge asked, his deep voice echoing throughout the deathly quiet courtroom.

"I felt the only way I could make an adequate evaluation of his condition was to recreate as closely as possible his mental condition at the time of the crime," Morrow explained. "I wanted to get inside his head, to get inside Mr. Garrow, and learn what mental state brought him to the point of taking another person's life."

"And did you learn that?"

"Yes. His chilling mental condition that day in the examining room corroborated my basic analysis that Mr. Garrow views people not as people, but as objects. For instance, the way he referred to having to kill 'it.' "

"No further questions, your honor," Belge stated. He walked back to the defense table and took his seat.

Judge Marthen asked the prosecution if they wished to cross-examine. Co-prosecutor Mordue spent over an hour trying to discredit Dr. Morrow's testimony before he scored any real points for the prosecution.

"Let me ask you, doctor," Mordue queried, "doesn't it bother you that the defendant, this man you have sworn has overwhelming mental deterioration, sits coiled in his wheelchair like an angry, dangerous misfit during testimony by the

various witnesses, yet chats amiably during recesses with reporters and law enforcement officers—even shows them newspaper clippings in which his picture appears?"

"Frankly, his behavior during this trial has confused me,"
Dr. Morrow answered.

Belge and Armani both winced noticeably.

"No further questions, your honor," a smiling Mordue concluded.

As Dr. Morrow stood to leave the witness chair, everyone's
attention in the courtroom was drawn to Garrow. The defendant looked up at Mordue, who was walking past his wheelchair, and said, "Keep smirking, you creep."

Mordue stopped in his tracks and stared down at Garrow.
Upon seeing the fearsome, hateful look on Garrow's face, the
prosecutor lost his smile.

Beginning the following morning, the prosecution presented
four psychiatrists to bolster their case. Doctors William Holt
and Walter Osinski, both from Albany, and doctors Francis
Durgin and Michael Boucher, both from Syracuse, testified
that Garrow was *not* mentally ill and *did* appreciate the nature
and consequences of his act of killing Philip Domblewski. Each
diagnosed Garrow as an antisocial personality with pathologi-
cal sexuality; each felt that Garrow conveniently forgot inci-
dents relating to his crime during his interviews with them in
order to fake mental illness. They testified that Garrow was a
liar and a malingerer and was acting as such to escape prosecution.

Belge's cross-examination of Dr. Osinski provided a moment
of excitement to balance the prosecution's chipping at Dr.
Morrow's testimony. Osinski was the court-appointed psychiatrist who had examined Garrow in 1961 after he had been arrested for the rape and assault that had sent him to prison for
eight years, and the same psychiatrist Armani had interviewed
months earlier. It was during that interview, when Osinski had
been reluctant to state that Garrow was suffering from mental
illness, that Armani's misgivings about using the psychiatrist as
a defense witness were confirmed. Armani's feeling that the
psychiatrist would prove to be an unsympathetic witness had
sprung to life during the period in which Garrow was at large
after the Domblewski murder, when Osinski leaked the results
of the 1961 examination to an *Albany Times-Union* reporter. In

the article, Osinski was quoted as stating that Garrow was not suffering from any mental disease, but rather was an antisocial personality. The clinical determination exactly matched Osinski's psychiatric evaluation of Garrow for the prosecution in this case.

Belge produced the cited *Albany Times-Union* edition and accused the psychiatrist of breaching his professional ethics regarding client confidentiality. In showing that Osinski had acted unethically by revealing confidential clinical information about Garrow, Belge succeeded in largely discrediting the Albany psychiatrist's testimony. He also planted the idea in the minds of the jurors that Osinski had made up his mind about Garrow's mental condition even before examining the defendant for this trial. Therefore, Belge concluded, Osinski was an unreliable, prejudiced witness whose testimony should be stricken from the record.

With that, both the prosecution and defense having presented their expert witnesses, it was time to hear the final arguments from each side. As the trial wound down into its last days, Garrow took an almost secondary role in the unfolding drama. Belge and Armani had been thrust fully into the spotlight. In addition to the arguments raging among the legal minds of the country as to whether Armani and Belge had acted legally and correctly in protecting their client's right of confidentiality, the Garrow case had become an international media event. Regular feature coverage appeared in *Time* and *Newsweek* magazines, in *The New York Times, Los Angeles Times, Chicago Tribune, Christian Science Monitor,* and other major national newspapers and in various European publications.

For the most part, Belge and Armani were vilified and condemned by the upstate New York press. Editorials, articles, and letters to the editor severely damned the two lawyers for not stepping forward with their knowledge of the location of the Hauck and Petz bodies. It would have spared the girls' parents the awful grief they suffered and saved taxpayers the hundreds of thousands of dollars expended by local and state law enforcement officers in their search for the girls' bodies.

National and international publications and news shows, on the other hand, tended to offer a more balanced, less strident viewpoint. The national media chose to debate the larger questions: At what point must a lawyer be compelled to violate his client's confidence? Can he violate it at all? And, in light of the lack of precedent in this area of the law, what are the exact limits of the sacred trust that exists between a client and attorney? Could these questions ever be fully and satisfactorily answered?

23

June 26–27, 1974

In his closing argument, Francis Belge produced an uproar in the courtroom. Headlines in countless newspapers reported his remarks to the jury that the wrong man was on trial in Lake Pleasant. Belge claimed that Robert Garrow's parents had warped their son's personality, and thus they were responsible in the truest sense for murdering Philip Domblewski. By chronically abusing and battering their son, the Garrows had created the insane person that was Robert Garrow, a man so mentally ill that he could not have understood the nature and consequences of his act of murdering Philip Domblewski. Belge completed his emotional appeal to the court by asking that Robert Garrow be sent to an institution for the criminally insane rather than to prison.

The prosecution summed up its case by attacking the credibility of the defense's psychiatric testimony. Norman Mordue pounded the idea home to the jury that Robert Garrow was indeed in complete control of his faculties on the morning of July 29, 1973, when he stole into the campsite, abducted the four young people, and killed Philip Domblewski. He argued that Garrow's motives were sexual, that the defendant intended to rape Carol Ann Freeman and murder her three male companions so there wouldn't be any witnesses. If help hadn't arrived from the Wells police, Mordue averred, Garrow would also have killed Nicholas Fiorello and David Freeman.

After more than two weeks of hearing both sides present their case, it was finally left to the jury to decide the fate of Robert Garrow. On June 27th, after less than two hours of deliberation, the jury found him guilty of first degree murder. The following day, he was sentenced by Judge Marthen to twenty-five years to life, the maximum sentence allowed by New York State law. Garrow's only comment before hearing his sentence pronounced was "I am sorry to have caused everyone so much trouble."

Following Garrow's sentencing, Belge and Armani were met on the courthouse steps by an army of news reporters. The two lawyers refused to respond to any questions about their alleged misconduct in the case. They simply stated that they would file an appeal to overturn Garrow's conviction. In answer to questions about the charges mounting against Garrow for murdering Daniel Porter, Susan Petz, and Alicia Hauck, the two lawyers offered no comment.

It was now up to Armani and Belge to dismantle their temporary office at Zeiser's Inn. When Belge disappeared that afternoon, the job fell to Armani, who loaded his car trunk full of law books and files. When he was done and ready to head back to Syracuse, Armani decided first to stop by the bar for a drink. He entered the spacious, wood-paneled taproom and immediately spotted Judge George Marthen, William Intemann, and Norman Mordue clustered together at one end of the bar. Armani walked directly up to the threesome.

"Let me buy you a drink, Frank," Hamilton County District Attorney Intemann offered.

"Sure. A beer," an exhausted Armani answered.

After John Zeiser, the inn's balding owner, set the bottle of Carling Black Label in front of him, Armani said loudly, "He's nuts, dammit. He's nuts, and you know it."

"Garrow is as sane as you and I," Mordue answered.

"I'm not talking about Garrow." Armani chug-a-lugged the beer straight from the bottle and banged the empty down hard on the bar. "I'm talking about Belge. He is wacko!"

With that Armani turned, walked out of Zeiser's, and climbed into his car.

During the two-hour drive home, Armani found himself devoid of the sense of fulfillment and relief he usually experienced at the end of any trial, whether he lost or won the case. His thoughts were centered on the work that lay ahead of him. He had to file Garrow's appeal. There was the matter of preparing his client's defense for the three murders Garrow had admitted to from the witness stand. Finally, he had to represent Garrow in the charges he faced on the eleven felony counts resulting from his abduction and sexual abuse of the two young girls the summer before in the town of Geddes.

The tasks facing him still in the forefront of his mind, Armani pulled into his driveway in the Syracuse suburb of Camillus a little after eight o'clock at night. The lights burning in the kitchen of his house were a welcoming beacon. It seemed like forever since he had spent a leisurely evening home with his family.

Dog-tired, Armani decided to wait until the following morning to haul his suitcases out of the trunk of his car. He walked to the back door of his house. The evening paper was still on the sidewalk, and the door was locked. This puzzled him. Mary looked forward to reading the *Herald Journal* before dinner and, since they lived in a semirural area in which there was hardly any crime, she rarely locked the doors at night.

Armani bent for the newspaper, unlocked the door, and walked into the deserted kitchen. A handwritten note was propped against the salt shaker in the center of the kitchen table.

Frank:
   I had a migraine and went to bed early. The girls are staying at friends' houses for the night. . . .

                                    Mary

So much for a leisurely evening home with my family, Armani thought. Too wound up to go to bed and suddenly grateful for this time alone in his house, he made himself a cup of instant coffee and sat down at the kitchen table to read the newspaper. The headline made his pulse quicken.

DISTRICT ATTORNEY SEEKS GRAND JURY INDICTMENT AGAINST GARROW LAWYERS

Armani lit a cigarette and read the copy. Onondaga County District Attorney Jon Holcombe was quoted as saying that

Belge and Armani had acted illegally and unprofessionally in withholding knowledge about the Hauck and Petz murders. Holcombe stated further that, by not disclosing the whereabouts of the girls' bodies to the authorities, Armani and Belge had violated the New York State law that guarantees the deceased a decent and humane burial. The district attorney had ordered the Syracuse police chief to launch an investigation into the matter for the purpose of seeking a grand jury indictment against Belge and Armani.

"Go ahead, bust my chops, Holcombe, you gloryhound," Armani said aloud.

He read down the page. Another article disturbed him even more. William Hauck, Alicia's father, was reported to have filed a petition with the New York State Bar Association to have Armani and Belge investigated and, hopefully, disbarred for their conduct in the Garrow case.

Armani shuddered at the realization that such a move could very well deny him his living. The bar association, the board regulating an attorney's professional conduct, had been known to be swayed in its disbarment proceedings by the opinions of powerful members of the legal community. And the majority of the legal community was clearly in solid opposition to the manner in which Armani and Belge had handled certain aspects of the Garrow case. Several nationally prominent attorneys had been quoted in articles in the *Los Angeles Times, Chicago Tribune,* and *New York Times* as severely critical of Armani and Belge.

Disgusted and anxious, Armani dropped the newspaper on the table, removed his glasses, and wiped them on his shirttail. He tried to imagine what it would be like not to be an attorney. The thought chilled him. Practicing law was all he knew.

Another article on the front page of the *Herald Journal* caught his eye. This one consisted of interviews with the parents of Alicia Hauck and Susan Petz. Both sets of parents were understandably bitter and outraged. They labeled Armani and Belge cruel and unfeeling. Mr. and Mrs. Petz were reported to be seeking legal redress against the two lawyers in their home state of Illinois.

Armani put the paper down. Feeling more exhausted than ever, he left the table, poured what remained of his coffee into the sink, and was about to leave the kitchen when Mary appeared. She was wearing a pale blue bathrobe, her hair was brushed, and the lines on her forehead indicated the pain her headache was causing her.

"Hi, Mary," Armani said warmly, his face showing a tired smile.

"Frank," she answered evenly.

"I thought you were in bed."

"I was, but I figured I could talk with you tonight as well as tomorrow," Mary said, moving across the kitchen in the direction of the door leading to the garage.

"I'm sure it could wait until morning. . . ." Armani's words trailed off. Mary had reached into the garage and brought back a light green bottle. The bottle was filled with an amber liquid, and there was a hunk of cloth protruding out the top.

"What! Where did you get that?" Armani asked, recognizing instantly that his wife was holding a Molotov Cocktail.

"I found it in the bushes behind the garage," she explained, placing the bottle on the counter.

"What kind of nut would put *that* near our house?" Armani asked, staring at the bottle.

"Probably the kind of nut who started that fire outside our garage last fall, Frank, just after your picture began appearing in the papers on the Garrow case."

"You can't say that, Mary," Armani reasoned. "The fire department said it could've been anything—a match, cigarette, anything—that started that fire."

"I asked the girls to stay at friends' tonight, Frank, because I'm afraid for them."

"C'mon now," Armani said unconvincingly. "There's nothing to worry about. That bottle of gasoline could've been left outside by some jerk who picked our house out at random."

"We both know that's not true. Besides this and that fire last year, there have been other instances when the girls and I have felt the hate that murderer has brought out in people."

"What are you talking about?" Armani asked.

Tears welled up in Mary's eyes. "Old friends ignore me. The phone hardly rings anymore, except for the obscene, hate calls."

"You've been getting those kinds of calls?" Frank asked. He had tried hard to keep this thing from directly affecting his family. He had deliberately not told his wife about the death threats he'd received or about the contract that had been taken out on his life.

"Hardly a day goes by that I don't get one of those calls. They use vile language and say all kinds of horrible things about you."

"Lousy bastards," Armani muttered.

"The girls have also been affected. Debbie had all kinds of trouble while she was at summer school at Oswego College. She would sit at a table in the cafeteria, and the other kids would get up and leave her to eat by herself. It got so bad that she dropped out of summer classes altogether. Dorina has been ridiculed by her friends because of what you did in the Garrow case."

"I'm sorry, Mary. I'm sorry that you and the girls have had to suffer because of this thing." He reached out his hand for hers. "I did the only thing I could. You have to believe that."

"And now this," his wife continued, withdrawing her hand from his and turning toward the Molotov Cocktail. "Who knows what will come next? I don't know how much longer I can stand it."

"It'll be okay," he said in an effort to comfort her.

"Is it done, Frank? Are you finished with that evil man?"

"Not yet. I have to defend Garrow on the other murders. Plus he'll appeal the Domblewski conviction." Armani skipped telling her about the battle he faced in defending himself against the charges piling up against him for his conduct in the case.

"Why can't you just back out?" she asked, her voice rising. "Let someone else take it from here."

"It doesn't work that way. I can't just quit. I've been appointed by the court to defend the man."

"Let them appoint someone else, then."

"They won't do that, Mary. The only way I could get out of the case is if I had some physical infirmity which would prevent me from carrying on. It's the law."

"The law! I'm so damned sick about hearing about the law! Haven't you done enough, Frank? You've given that man nearly a year of your life. Your family has suffered because of it. Isn't that enough?"

Armani listened.

"This case has taken all of your time and energy. We haven't made any money since you've been involved with Garrow. Debbie's in college, and Dorina goes next year. We won't have enough money to pay their expenses."

"I'm getting paid for my work on the Garrow case," Armani responded weakly.

"Sure! I read in the paper how much you were paid. Eight thousand dollars! Great! You probably spent that much just in motel and phone bills since you began working on the case. How much money were the court reporters paid, Frank?"

"The three of them split ninety thousand dollars," he answered sheepishly.

"You think *that's* just?"

"It's the way it is."

His wife shook her head slowly.

"C'mon, Mary. Let's go upstairs to bed. We're both tired. We can talk about this thing some more tomorrow if you like."

Mary glanced once again at the Molotov Cocktail, then turned back to her husband. "No more talk, Frank. I won't expose the girls to this kind of danger any longer."

"If it'll make you feel better, I'll get someone to watch the house."

"No! That's not enough. I'm taking Debbie and Dorina to live with my parents for a while."

"Please, Mary. Don't go," he pleaded. "I need you."

"Need me? C'mon, Frank. We haven't been a family since you started this case. You don't need us. You need all the attention you've been getting from the papers and TV. You're obsessed with this thing; it's like a drug to you. And that doesn't leave anything for the girls and me."

"I wish you would just hold on for a couple more months," he persisted feebly. Armani knew that Mary, although extremely patient about most things, rarely changed her mind once she had become convinced about something.

"I can't stay, Frank. I have to leave—for the girls, and for me. I'll not have them damaged further because of this. As it is, they are practically nervous wrecks. And so am I." With that, she walked out of the kitchen and began climbing the stairs.

Armani waited a few moments before heading upstairs. He was thinking about what Mary had said about him being hooked on this case, about how he was trapped into staying with Garrow because of the publicity and the fame. She was right, of course. At least, that was the reason up to this point. What his wife didn't realize was that he was now tied fast to Garrow for another reason: His reputation and his right to practice law were on the line. He couldn't bail out even if he wanted to. He was in too deep.

24

June 28, 1974

THE FOLLOWING MORNING, Armani silently endured the anguish of watching his wife and daughters pack suitcases and drive away in the family station wagon. Afterward, he took his time showering and dressing. The sense of urgency that had propelled him over the past year was gone. He felt tired and depressed and without purpose.

He unloaded his personal gear from the Mercedes, talked to a sheriff's deputy dispatched to the house in response to Armani's call about the Molotov Cocktail, then drove to downtown Syracuse. He had to stop by the courthouse to pick up a copy of the murder indictment against Garrow in the Hauck case, so he could begin preparing his client's defense.

The June day was turning into a scorcher when Armani emerged from the courthouse at eleven o'clock. He decided on an early lunch at the Hotel Syracuse before driving the five miles to his office. While walking to the hotel, Armani paused at the Columbus Circle fountain. He was watching the dancing streams of water, when John Prizzuti, a local plumber and long-time client, joined him at the fountain. Prizzuti didn't seem to notice who was standing beside him.

"Johnny!" Armani reached out his hand. "How's it going?"

The calm look on his face transforming into disgust and his brown eyes burning with anger, Prizzuti refused the lawyer's handshake. "If it would've been my daughter, Armani, I would have killed you."

"Hold it a second, Johnny," a stunned Armani called.

Prizzuti stepped away from the fountain, then turned and said, "And you ain't gettin' any more of my legal business."

Armani took a deep breath to calm himself, then turned away from the fountain. To reach the Hotel Syracuse, he had to pass the Catholic cathedral. He slowed his step at the front entrance of the church. Maybe he would go in to say a few prayers. He quickly dismissed that idea, figuring it would be a form of spiritual panhandling.

After lunch, he drove to his office, where he was greeted with more bad news. Clients had been sending letters by the droves, condemning him for his behavior in the Garrow case and announcing that they were firing him as their lawyer.

This flurry of business loss didn't help his frame of mind when he read over his firm's financial report, which his secretary had left on his desk. Even someone as unschooled in such matters as Armani quickly recognized the signs of impending financial disaster. As it stood, there wasn't going to be enough money at the end of the month to meet his payroll. He made a mental note to transfer some money out of his personal account to keep his law office afloat. Then he wondered if, given the sharp drop in business, the accounts receivable would provide adequate funds so he could meet the following month's payroll and expenses. He made himself put it out of his mind. He would worry about next month next month.

To top off Armani's day, Francis Belge decided to drop by to talk with him.

"Where the hell did you disappear to after Garrow's sentencing?" Armani demanded when Belge stepped into his private office.

"Figured I'd better scram quick after my immunity ran out," Belge answered. He lowered himself into the chair facing Armani's desk. "A few people in Lake Pleasant would have liked to see me in the cell next to Garrow's."

"No doubt," Armani agreed, thinking about how the townspeople had begun to tire of Belge's antics outside the courtroom. There had been talk among the deputy sheriffs of trying to pin something on Belge after the trial was completed.

"Will you tell me what the hell *this* is all about?" Armani tossed the morning paper across the desk. The headlines screamed that Francis Belge was bringing charges against the Onondaga County district attorney. "Are you serious about trying to lock Holcombe up?"

Belge's eyes twinkled. "Absolutely! I even convinced a Hamilton County justice of the peace to issue a warrant for Holcombe's arrest."

"On what charge?" an astonished Armani asked.

"Obstructing justice on the day he shot his mouth off in the courtroom and for his news releases during the trial."

"You gotta be outta your melon, Belge," Armani said. "Sure as hell they'll throw that one out."

"We'll see," Belge answered. "In the meantime, the warrant will give him something to think about besides coming after us."

Armani laughed.

"What are we going to do about Garrow's appeal, Frank?" Belge asked, growing more serious.

"For openers, we cite our request for a change of venue out of Hamilton County being turned down. As proof of pretrial community prejudice against our client, we show how we had to poll over seventy-five percent of the county's residents to get a jury."

"Also hit on the fact that the jury averaged over sixty-two years in age," Belge added. "That geriatric set definitely wasn't a jury of Garrow's peers."

"In addition," Armani continued, "we should attack the veracity of the prosecution's psychiatric testimony. That all four of their shrinks consulted with one another and came up with an identical diagnosis raises a serious question."

"Good." Belge grew excited. "Okay, how are we going to proceed on the Porter, Petz, and Hauck cases?"

"Those are easy. We plead him guilty to all three murders."

"Guilty?"

"He admitted the killings in the courtroom. Remember?" Armani's anger toward Belge was still strong.

"We go for innocent by reason of insanity on all three killings," Belge said.

"No way. We plead Garrow guilty to the Hauck, Petz, and Porter killings so we can make a deal for him to draw concurrent sentences. If we try the cases and lose, you can bet the rent that the judges, just out of spite for having to hear the cases, will give Garrow consecutive sentences."

"That's stupid, and you know it," Belge countered. "The man's insane. We both know that."

"So what do we do with the Domblewski verdict? You think another jury would go out on a limb and find Garrow innocent by reason of insanity on the Petz, Porter, or Hauck murders? If they did, in essence they would be claiming that the Hamilton County jury was wrong."

"That's exactly why we should try the Hauck, Petz, and Porter cases *before* we appeal the Domblewski verdict. We stand a much better chance of winning the appeal if we can get Garrow off on one of those other three killings. Way I see it, we better our odds by trying those three cases instead of knuckling under and pleading Garrow guilty."

"Garrow informed me that he won't go to trial in Syracuse on the Hauck case," Armani replied. "He doesn't want his family to go through more hell because of the publicity."

"So we go for a change of venue on the Hauck case," Belge countered.

"Right. Holcombe's not gonna let that publicity plum out of his hands. He'll be calling in every favor owed him to block a change of venue. My mind's made up."

"What if I told you that Garrow wants just me to represent him from here on out?" Belge asked, looking Armani hard in the eyes.

Armani's nostrils flared. "Garrow said that?"

"He called me from Dannemora this morning."

"Well, you can just tell that creep that it's okay with me. This thing has kicked my butt enough anyway." Armani was hurt and angry.

"No need to go off the edge, Frank," Belge admonished. "He only said he was *thinking* about having me go it alone, since I'm the one with the most trial experience."

"What's your strategy, Belge? Have him admit some additional murders from the stand?"

"How many times do I have to tell you that bringing Garrow on the stand as our first witness was our only shot. We had to shock that senile jury into considering our argument; they already had their minds made up. Even Judge Marthen admitted that it was a brilliant tactic."

"Why the hell wouldn't he?" Armani snorted. "Marthen *never* bought our insanity defense."

"Okay," Belge said. "I can see that there's no reasoning with you. I'll be up at Henderson Harbor if you want me."

"Don't wait by the phone."

"You might change your mind about calling me," Belge said on his way out of the office. "Read tonight's paper. I've filed formal charges with the New York Bar to have Holcombe disbarred for his unethical conduct in the Garrow case."

"What!" Armani blurted. "You drop a salvo like that and leave town? The reporters will be all over me tomorrow for a response."

"You've got my phone number. Besides, Frank, I thought you liked being in the big time." Belge finger-saluted Armani, then walked out the door.

"Oh, man. As if this thing isn't complicated enough." Armani slowly expelled a long breath. "Belge blows through town like a tornado, and I get to pick up the pieces."

Armani dragged himself out of his office at five that afternoon. On the way home he developed a pounding headache and felt an uncomfortable sensation in his chest. Indigestion, no doubt. He would take a couple of aspirins and an Alka-Seltzer before eating.

When he turned onto his street, he noticed that his father's red pickup truck was parked in his driveway. Armani wondered what the old man was doing there. Ezzelino Armani almost never stopped over unless he called first. As the attorney climbed from his car, his father, seventy-five years old and in robust health, walked over to greet him. Ezzelino Armani, his complexion resembling weathered leather, had a lionlike mane of white hair and slate-colored eyes that could bore holes in plate steel.

Armani's attention was drawn immediately to the hunting rifle his father was carrying. "Is something wrong, Dad?"

"I know about Mary." There was loving concern in the old man's eyes, but his face was grim. "She called the house."

"Yeah," Armani said forlornly. "What the hell was I supposed to do? She wouldn't listen."

"I know. The women get *pazzo*—crazy in the head—sometimes." His father cracked a knowing smile.

"But why the gun?" Armani asked.

"I've come to protect your house."

"You what?"

"Those hoodlums who did this thing last night might be back. Or there could be others."

"Dad, please. I'm in no danger. The police promised me they would keep an eye on the place."

"Eh!" His father gestured with his free hand. "They have more to do than protect you and your property full-time. I stay here with you for a few days."

"Believe me, Dad, I'll be all right."

"And I said I'm staying, Francesco."

"What about Mom?"

"Her sister will stay at the house while I'm over here. Be good for her; she's been lonely since her husband died. Now, what about dinner? I'm hungry."

Secretly glad for the company, Armani smiled widely and shook his head. He put his arm around his father's shoulder, and the two men headed for the kitchen door.

"Can you still whip up a mean frittata?" Frank asked.

"The best, Francesco, the best," the old man answered, smiling. He stood aside while his son unlocked the door.

After dinner, while his son slept and as he would do each night for two weeks, Ezzelino Armani stationed himself in the living room of Frank's house. His hunting rifle across his thighs, the old man stood guard until dawn.

During the morning hours, while Frank was away at his office, Ezzelino, his rifle next to him, rested in the guest room. He generally awoke sometime in the early afternoon, fixed something to eat, then busied himself with yard work until his son returned home. The old man also answered the phone in his son's absence. The number of crank threatening calls he received gave Ezzelino an idea of the pressure his son was under. Even after Armani changed his number to an unlisted one, the calls still came, though less frequently.

25

January 1975

ARMANI HAD DONE EVERYTHING he could to stay awake during the four-hour drive to Dannemora State Prison. Since the previous summer, after Garrow changed his mind and indicated that he wanted Armani to continue to represent him, and after Belge faded from the case, the lawyer had frequently made this trip to confer with his client about some aspect of the Hauck, Porter, and Petz cases and about the appeal on the Domblewski conviction, which the lawyer had filed some months earlier. He was fatigued by the time he reached Dannemora, but mildly excited, too. He had come up with a plan that he believed could dispose of the three murder indictments before they were brought to trial.

Built in the 1840s in what could best be labeled as fortress style, Dannemora State Prison was comprised of several imposing gray stone buildings. The prison compound was surrounded by a twenty-foot-high stone wall intermittently spotted with guard towers.

Armani eased his car to a halt in front of the administration building. Once in the anteroom off the visitors' lounge, Armani lit a cigarette, walked to the heavily barred window, and looked out. Except for a few hardy inmates jogging through the snow squalls, the prison exercise area was deserted. Beyond the exercise area, against the wall and under the roof overhang of one of the buildings, huddled clusters of gray-suited inmates, dancing in place and stamping their feet to stay warm.

Whoever had named this place a correctional facility had to have been joking. Dannemora was a holding pen that offered make-work jobs to keep the inmates busy, nothing more. What skills a man did pick up here, he learned from other inmates— skills that would help him resume his life of crime once he got out. Eighty percent of those released from Dannemora eventually returned to prison. All most inmates learned was how to be better at being bad.

The door behind him swung open. Armani turned around. A guard pushed Robert Garrow into the room. Though still in a wheelchair, Garrow looked stronger and more fit than he had at the trial. He wore only a white sock on his left foot. His left arm, however, was withered and glazed, and the fingers on his left hand were clawed.

Garrow waited until the guard had left the room, then greeted Armani. He wheeled himself to a spot at the oak table in the middle of the room.

"Feeling okay, Bob?" Armani asked as he shook Garrow's hand.

"My foot hurts real bad. But other than that, I'm all right."

"Your wife been up to see you lately?" Armani asked politely, as he removed a sheaf of papers from his briefcase.

"She comes up once a week, on Saturday. She's working, you know."

"I heard," Armani said absent-mindedly. "Now look, Bob, I think I've worked out a deal on the Porter, Petz, and Hauck charges, one you'll like."

Garrow rested his chin on his right palm and waited.

"I finally got the Onondaga and Essex County DAs to go along with plea bargaining the cases. Holcombe fought like hell against it at first. He wanted you to fry. But now he's willing to play ball with us in order to save the taxpayers the money of putting you on trial."

"What's the deal?" Garrow asked, looking up.

"We plead you guilty to second degree murder in all three cases, and you get concurrent fifteen-to-life sentences. This deal would also cover all the other outstanding charges against you, including the incident involving the two girls in Geddes, the seven rapes you confessed to committing, and the charges resulting from the manhunt. So it works out that you only serve the time you got for the Domblewski murder."

"When would I be eligible for parole?"

"The same as now—in twenty-five years," Armani answered.

"How about me getting transferred out of here to Fishkill, so I can get medical and psychiatric treatment?" Garrow asked. Fishkill was the state's medium security medical-psychiatric facility, located near Newburgh.

"Nothing definite on that yet, Bob. I'm seeing what I can do. And how about on your end? You write that letter requesting transfer to Fishkill like I told you to do?"

"Last week, to Commissioner of Corrections Hongisto." Garrow then added, "I have to get out of here, Frank. Any number of guys in this joint would like to stick a knife in my back."

"Believe me when I say that if you cooperate on this plea bargain, you'll stand a good chance of getting to Fishkill," Armani reassured him.

"I don't know, Frank. Something tells me to fight those murder charges."

"That would, in my opinion, be a foolish move, Bob. It'll be tough to get any jury to find you insane, especially after the way the Domblewski verdict came down."

"So you think I should take this offer?"

"I believe it's a helluva package. Like I said, by going for it, your sentence stays the same. Fight the Porter, Petz, and Hauck charges, and you risk adding more time to your sentences."

"How's the plea bargain affect my appeal?"

"If we're lucky enough to get a reversal on the Domblewski verdict, based on the insanity plea, we'll then appeal the other charges based on the same grounds. You're insane in one, you gotta be insane in the other three."

"Let me think about it, Frank," Garrow answered pensively.

"I need your answer within a week." Armani began gathering his things. "The district attorneys aren't going to sit still for long. They've got pressure on them to act on your cases. Holcombe, especially, could back out at any time."

"I'll let you know within a week."

"Take care, Bob," Armani said. He picked up his briefcase and turned to knock on the door to be let out.

"Frank?"

"Yeah?"

"Just so you know, I been exercising my arm and leg," Garrow announced. A smile playing on his lips, he slowly lifted himself from the wheelchair until he stood facing Armani.

"Exercising? I thought . . . !" an astonished Armani blurted. After eighteen months of seeing Garrow in a sitting position, he had forgotten how big and powerful-looking his client was.

"I work out late at night, when everybody's asleep. I do one-legged deep-knee bends and have a little rubber ball I squeeze," Garrow explained. He lowered himself to the floor and effortlessly reeled off a set of ten one-armed push-ups. Red-faced, he looked up at Armani and added, "I'm gettin' real strong, Frank."

"I can see that," Armani answered nervously as he watched Garrow get back to his feet. He didn't like being in the room alone with a mobile Garrow.

"I'm going to try and make it out of here."

"You're nuts," Armani replied without thinking, then wished he had phrased it differently. The last thing he wanted to do was to agitate Garrow at that moment.

"I've got a plan," Garrow said, obviously enjoying surprising Armani like this.

"Hold it, Bob," Armani directed, forgetting his apprehension for the instant. He stepped across the room until he stood face-to-face with Garrow. "I don't want to hear anything about it. There's no confidentiality between us with that kind of information. If what you're telling me involves committing a crime, I'm legally bound to report it."

"Yeah, of course, Frank. See you later," Garrow said. With a smile on his face, he lowered himself back into his wheelchair. "Go ahead and knock. I'm ready."

Once Garrow was back in the wheelchair, all the power seemed to drain out of him. He was back to being the helpless inmate.

Armani knocked on the door, and the guard let him out of the anteroom. While walking through the series of iron gates to the prison lobby and outside into the worsening snowstorm, Armani wondered whether Garrow was actually serious about trying to escape. He even paused to consider going back inside to report Garrow's threat to the prison authorities. He decided against it when he remembered how Garrow had talked of escaping from the Hamilton County jail on numerous occasions during his trial without ever trying. Figuring Garrow's latest threat for more idle, grandiose talk, Armani dismissed it from his mind.

26

February 1975

ARMANI ENTERED HIS OFFICE and headed for the automatic
telephone answering machine he had purchased after laying off
the last of his five legal secretaries. Over the past months his
business had dwindled to practically nothing, and he had also
had to let his three associate lawyers go. His lone employee was
a part-time legal secretary who came in three afternoons a week
to do typing and filing.

Armani listened to the previous day's calls and listed them
on the writing pad next to the phone. Nothing urgent. He
would return the calls later that day.

He made a pot of coffee on the automatic drip machine and
carried a mugful into his private office. The stack of files on his
desk made him wince—lots of cases to close out, cases for which
he had already been paid. There wasn't a newly opened one
among the batch. He wondered if he would make it through
February to March as an attorney.

With more impending problems to deal with today, he tried
pushing his feelings of financial insecurity to the back of his
mind. He had to pick up some data at his office, then drive to
the airport. Elliot Taikeff, the highly regarded lawyer from
New York City who had agreed to defend Armani at today's
grand jury hearing on his conduct in the Garrow case, was ar-
riving within the hour. Taikeff had stepped forward to repre-

sent Armani after being urged to do so by Dean Howard Grant, who was currently out of the country.

Armani took a moment to enjoy his cup of coffee and to smoke a cigarette. He could feel the tension in his stomach and the perspiration soaking his shirt under his arms. It was all on the line for him today. It was probably the single most important day of his legal career. His right to practice law hung in the balance of this morning's grand jury hearing. If the grand jury returned an indictment against him, their decision would certainly affect the outcome of the state bar association's investigation into whether Armani had acted properly in protecting his client's right to confidentiality in the Alicia Hauck and Susan Petz murder cases.

Armani felt good that an attorney of Taikeff's caliber and reputation had volunteered his services for today's proceedings. Elliot Taikeff was one of the few nationally prominent lawyers who hadn't vilified Armani for his stand in the Garrow case, either in the press or in articles published in various legal journals. Further, so important did Taikeff consider the issue of client-lawyer confidentiality at stake in today's grand jury probe that he had made it clear to Armani that he would accept no payment for defending him. Armani had had to eat his pride to accept Taikeff's free legal aid.

Armani hadn't been able to count much on Francis Belge's cooperation in preparing for today's grand jury hearing. Belge had been spending his time and energy in a public feud with Onondaga District Attorney Jon Holcombe. Hardly a day had passed without some article in the newspapers detailing a new charge one had hurled against the other. Having had little communication with Belge about today's hearing, Armani had no idea how Belge was going to handle the charges against him. In the press, Belge had repeatedly labeled the charges as trumped up against him by Holcombe to discredit the suits Belge had brought against the Onondaga district attorney.

Armani smiled at the thought of Belge's tactic of staying on the offensive. Belge kept firing salvos at his opponents so that they were so busy defending themselves they didn't have time to retake the offensive. Like Belge or not, Armani thought, you had to admire his spunk. The guy lived life as if he had nothing to lose.

Armani checked his watch. Time to go. He gathered the necessary documents into his briefcase, flipped on the phone answering machine, and headed out of his office.

Twenty minutes later he parked his Mercedes near the Hancock Airport terminal and walked inside. He arrived at the gate just in time to meet Elliot Taikeff coming out of the tunnel. Taikeff walked with purposeful confidence and greeted Armani with a handshake.

"Ready to go to court?" Taikeff asked as the two men turned toward the main terminal. The patrician-looking, gray-haired attorney wore a fashionable blue pin-striped three-piece suit. His brown eyes were partly obscured by tinted, gold-rimmed glasses that rode a bit low on his thin, curved nose.

"Ready as I'll ever be," Armani answered, feeling less nervous now that Taikeff had arrived. "Any luggage?"

"Just this," the New York attorney said. He held his carry-on suitcase out in front of him. In his other, well-manicured hand was a thin leather briefcase.

Once in Armani's car, Taikeff remarked, "Saw in the *Times* that Garrow is suing you for denying him due process in the Domblewski case."

"For five million dollars." Armani laughed. It was an amount of money so out of his reality that he really hadn't connected with the full implications of the lawsuit. "I'm not the only one. He's suing Holcombe for three million and Belge for two."

"Guess he figured you were more of an obstructionist than the others," Taikeff said. He smiled, showing even, well-tended teeth.

"How the hell do you figure a guy like that?" Armani added. "He's also suing the state for ten million. Claims he received improper medical treatment for the gunshot wounds he sustained when captured."

"Also read where he fired you as his attorney," Taikeff continued.

"He fired me, all right. Then, three days later, he petitioned the court to have me reinstated as his attorney."

"How did the court rule?"

"That I had had enough of Robert Garrow. They assigned him another lawyer to handle his appeal. Didn't matter much, anyway. I'd already plea bargained the other murder charges against him, so my work was essentially finished."

"Would you have stayed with the case if the court had reappointed you, Frank?"

"Let's just say that the court answered my prayers when they appointed him another attorney."

They made the rest of the drive into Syracuse in silence. Armani thought back to five weeks earlier, when he had received word that Garrow had fired him and was suing him for denying him due process. Initially, Armani had taken it personally. He had felt hurt and betrayed—Garrow was ungrateful for all the sacrifices his attorney had made for him. He had believed that Garrow was robbing him of something, purposefully denying Armani the right to complete the process that he had begun nearly two years earlier. This resentment had been shortlived, however, soon replaced by the elation of finally being finished with Robert Garrow. Whatever residual indignation he might have felt over the way Garrow had turned on him soon disappeared. The day after Garrow's announcement that he had fired his attorneys and was suing them had hit the papers was the day that Armani's wife and two daughters moved back into the family home. Armani had missed them terribly. In their absence, he had fully realized how important his family was to him.

It was nine-fifteen when Armani eased his Mercedes into the Onondaga County courthouse parking lot. The two men climbed out of the car. They approached the knot of reporters waiting outside the courthouse. Taikeff leaned to him and said, "Not a word to these people, Frank. You'll do your talking inside."

Armani obeyed orders and walked silently through the reporters' barrage of questions.

Once outside the grand jury room, the two attorneys paused.

"You know the law says that I must leave before your testimony," Taikeff said. "But I want you to understand that, at any time, if you need counsel about any point or are afraid of prejudicing your testimony while responding to any of the DA's questions, you can call for a recess. You're allowed to come out of the courtroom to consult with me."

"I've got a lot of fear about going in there," Armani confessed.

"You're going to be walking a thin tightrope, Frank. You

must be careful not to violate either your client's or Belge's confidence. Plus you must be cautious that the prosecution doesn't set some kind of trap for you, doesn't force you to implicate yourself. You have done nothing wrong and shouldn't be concerned. The facts will speak for themselves."

Armani smiled weakly, checked his watch, and said, "Guess I'd better get in there."

Taikeff reached out and took Armani's arm. "Every lawyer who's worth his salt is proud of you."

They entered the courtroom. The grand jury was seated, the District Attorney Jon Holcombe and Norman Mordue were waiting at the prosecutor's table. Armani nodded to Holcombe and Mordue and took a seat in the front row.

Within seconds Judge Ormand Gale, Onondaga County Court judge, stepped out of his chambers and took his seat behind the elevated bench. Short and elflike, with conservatively cut steel gray hair and a pinched but kindly face, Gale was regarded as an eminently fair jurist.

"The Onondaga County Grand Jury is in session," the bailiff called.

"The purpose of this hearing," Judge Gale advised, "is not to establish the guilt or innocence of either Mr. Belge or Mr. Armani. It is to get to the facts and to decide whether there is enough evidence of criminal behavior against one or both of these attorneys to warrant an indictment. If this grand jury elects to hand down an indictment, either Mr. Belge or Mr. Armani, or both of them, will have their day in court to defend themselves against whatever charges might be brought against them. Now, are the people ready to proceed?"

"The people are ready," Jon Holcombe answered.

"Are Misters Belge and Armani ready?" Judge Gale asked, peering over his reading glasses.

"Mr. Armani is ready," Taikoff announced. "The grand jury has been unable to serve Mr. Belge with a subpoena," Holcombe stated.

A puzzled Judge Gale glanced up from the papers on his desk.

"He's supposed to be out of the country," the bailiff continued. "All efforts to locate him have failed."

If Belge was out of the country, Armani mused, he had probably ridden the ferry across the St. Lawrence into Canada for the day. Armani was amazed that his colleague had had the nerve to ignore this grand jury hearing.

"And now," Judge Gale said, "according to the rules of this court I must excuse myself from this inquiry, and I direct that the District Attorney conduct this hearing pursuant to my instruction." Judge Gale and Elliot Taikoff left the grand jury room.

Instead of Holcombe, Assistant District Attorney Norman Mordue moved to the front of the courtroom. "The people call Frank H. Armani," he said.

Armani pushed from his seat and walked slowly to the witness stand. As he did, he thought, Those can't be butterflies in my stomach; they feel like pigeons.

"You are Frank H. Armani?" Mordue asked for the record.

"Yes, sir."

"And you're from West Genesee Street, Syracuse, New York—that's your law office?"

"That's my law office."

Mordue walked to the prosecution table and brought back a couple of documents. "Mr. Armani, I have here exhibits 5 and 5A. These are waivers of immunity before the grand jury?"

"Yes, I'm going to waive immunity, as I would like the grand jury to know that in my mind I feel I have done nothing wrong," Armani stated. Taikeff had warned Armani that waiving the immunity to which he was entitled at this grand jury hearing was a dangerous, all-or-nothing tactic, one that could backfire. But Armani had insisted upon doing it this way. He wanted to pull out all stops to clear his name once and for all.

"Sign exhibit 5, please."

Armani signed the waiver of immunity, as did the grand jury foreman.

With that formality out of the way, the bailiff swore Armani in as a witness. Mordue was replaced in the front of the courtroom by Onondaga County District Attorney Jon Holcombe.

"Mr. Armani, would you state your age please?" Holcombe asked in a strong voice.

"Forty-seven."

Holcombe then went on to ask Armani questions about his educational and professional background, questions to which Armani gave direct, though slightly nervous answers.

"Can you tell us the date that you were so engaged or employed or retained to represent a person by the name of Robert Garrow on a murder charge?" Holcombe picked up.

"My recollection is that it was on the day of arraignment, at that time or by phone conversation prior to that. Approximately August of 1973." Armani struggled to remember exact details. So much had happened in the intervening months since he had agreed to undertake Garrow's defense.

Holcombe, sensing Armani's nervousness, pounded away at him with a barrage of questions for the next hour. The district attorney was attempting with his deft, probing questions to lead Armani into admitting that he or Belge had acted unethically to maintain their client's confidentiality in connection with the murder of Alicia Hauck. Holcombe cross-examined Armani about details of the ill-fated plea bargaining attempt in which Armani and Belge had tried to trade information about the Hauck girl's murder for a guarantee that Garrow would be placed in a mental institution rather than prison. He queried the attorney about Belge's public statement that he had gone without Armani to Oakwood Cemetery, reassembled the Hauck girl's remains and photographed them. Holcombe asked about the whereabouts of the photograph, as well as the tapes of the two attorneys' conversations with Garrow relating to the Alicia Hauck murder, and Armani admitted that he had destroyed them. Holcombe dug for every detail about Armani's professional conduct in protecting Robert Garrow's confidentiality. Holcombe seemed almost more familiar with them than did Armani, running down details about the manhunt, the trial, and the aftermath. In fact, Armani came off rather poorly in his testimony. He had to reverse himself several times as he struggled to remember times, dates, people, and places.

But there was one unshakable core issue on which Armani held firm: He and Belge had done nothing unethical or illegal by maintaining their client's right to confidentiality with his attorney. Armani was able to get across the point that he and Belge, in remaining silent about the information Garrow had shared with them regarding the fate of Alicia Hauck, Susan Petz, and Daniel Porter, had upheld the sacred trust between an attorney and his client that is guaranteed by the Constitution and by a lawyer's code of professional ethics.

Holcombe, having completed his cross-examination, turned

toward the prosecution table and said, "No further questions. You're excused."

Armani, drained but anxious, replied, "I would like to make a statement."

Holcombe kept his eyes on the papers spread across the table and repeated, "No further questions. You're excused."

Armani began sweating more profusely, and there was an edge to his voice when he asked, "Mr. Foreman, may I make a statement?"

The grand jury foreman, a smallish man with gray hair and pointed features, answered, "No."

District Attorney Holcombe, glancing over at Armani, who was about to leave the witness stand, nodded. Then, as if sympathizing with Armani's plight, he said, "Go ahead and make your statement, Mr. Armani."

Frank Armani faced the twenty-five jurors. Speaking with considerable emotion, he began, "I know it's dangerous for a lawyer to make statements in his own defense. I know that, but I just want you people to understand that I realize how Alicia Hauck's parents feel. I know I don't blame them; I understand exactly what they're going through, if it's possible for anyone to understand that. But God only knows that this thing drove me crazy; it really bothered me. And if there was any way I could have, I would have told Mr. and Mrs. Hauck. But my hands were tied. And, as a result, this thing has cost me dearly. My law practice failed. I spent nearly forty thousand dollars defending Garrow, for which I was reimbursed eight thousand for my services by the court. I've lost about every friend I have. *But there was nothing else I could do. Please believe that.*"

His throat closing from the emotion he felt, Armani stepped slowly from the witness stand and returned to his seat.

The foreman said in a soft voice, "The witness is excused."

With that Armani headed out of the grand jury room and left his fate to the fifteen people in the jury box.

"How'd you do?" Taikeff, waiting anxiously in the hallway, asked.

"I make a better lawyer than I do a witness," Armani said. He smiled wanly. "Let's go get something to eat. I'll tell you all about it on the way."

They walked the several blocks to the Hotel Syracuse, Taikeff doing most of the listening and Armani recounting the hearing as best he could to the New York City attorney. The two attorneys weren't seated an hour—one of the longest of Armani's life—before the Syracuse lawyer was summoned to the phone. Judge Gale's law clerk was on the line.

Armani wasn't gone from the table long enough for Taikeff to finish his coffee. The New York City attorney watched Armani walk back across the crowded room toward him. By the lightness of Armani's step and by the broad grin on his face, Taikeff guessed immediately what the verdict had been.

"So?" Taikeff asked.

"They voted no bill on me," Armani answered, lowering himself into the heavily padded chair. He removed a scrap of paper from his jacket pocket and read from it. "Judge Gale issued this summation: 'The effectiveness of counsel is only as great as the confidentiality of its client-attorney relationship. If the lawyer cannot get all the facts about the case because his client fears that those facts can be divulged later to the press or the authorities, he can only give his client half of a defense.' "

"Great!" Taikeff exclaimed. His enthusiasm melted away when he saw the smile leave Armani's lips. "What's wrong, Frank?"

"I may have been cleared of all charges, but they've voted to indict Belge on two counts of violating the health law that guarantees the deceased a speedy and humane burial."

His brow showing his puzzlement, Taikeff sipped his coffee. Then he asked, "Why Belge and not you?"

"I can't figure it either," Armani said, reaching for a piece of bread. "Unless they considered that by going back to Oakwood Cemetery and reassembling the body to photograph it, he somehow went further than I did."

"Must be," Taikeff added. "Of course you feel badly for Belge. But, Frank, I'd like to toast you on your moment of vindication. You won a crucial victory for all of us in there today."

"And to you, for helping to pull me out of the fire," Armani responded.

Taikeff lifted his cup and toasted Armani. Armani returned the gesture with his coffee cup, then paused, holding his cup out in front of his face as if readying to say something. Suddenly he broke into a drenching sweat. His lips pulled back into a grimace, and he dropped his cup to the table, splashing coffee all over himself and Taikeff. His face tensed, then contorted. His eyes bulged and his complexion turned the color of clammy slate.

Once over the immediate shock of being splashed with hot coffee, an alarmed Taikeff asked, "What is it, Frank?"

Armani responded with gasping, choking noises. His hand crept slowly up his chest. He tried ripping his collar free from his throat. With his other hand, he grabbed at the left side of his chest.

"Please, somebody, help!" Taikeff cried out, bolting to his feet and moving to Armani's side. "Someone call an ambulance. This man is having a heart attack."

27

September 8, 1978

It was late evening. Faint light from a nearby hallway exit sign fell across Robert Garrow, who was awake and lying under the covers of his bed. He was thinking how much he liked his room at Fishkill, formerly Mattewan Prison for the criminally insane and now a medium security correctional facility for elderly and handicapped prisoners. With real furniture, a private bathroom, and plaster walls, it was far less austere and depressing than were his cells at Dannemora or Auburn, where he had been sent last year after his life had been threatened.

Garrow had been extremely surprised when, a couple of months before, he had been advised that he was being transferred to Fishkill. After over four years of seeing his transfer requests ignored by the Department of Corrections, Garrow had been convinced that he would serve out his term in either Dannemora or Auburn. Just when he had about given up hope of ever making it to Fishkill, he was paid a visit by a Department of Corrections official from Albany. The state wanted to put an end to the bad publicity being kicked up by Garrow's $10 million lawsuit against New York State. In the suit, Garrow charged the state police and the BCI with brutality and also claimed that he had received improper medical treatment for the wounds he had sustained when captured in 1973. According to the Department of Corrections official who visited him, all Garrow had to do to be transferred to Fishkill was to withdraw his suit and make a public statement extolling the quality of medical and psychiatric treatment he expected to receive at the medium security facility near Newburgh. Of course, Garrow had jumped at the offer. But he had reasons other than his personal comfort and safety and desire for rehabilitation for wanting to be at Fishkill.

Lying on his back in bed, he checked his watch. The luminous dial read quarter to twelve. Fully clothed, Garrow slid quietly out from under the covers. He jammed his hand between the mattress and spring of his bed into the small incision he had made in the mattress and removed the .32 caliber Gaztanaga Destroyer pistol from its hiding place. It had been so easy for his nineteen-year-old son to smuggle the gun in to him. Robert, Jr., had simply buried the pistol in a bucket of fried chicken and carried it past the guards—easy as that.

Garrow then reached under the metal bed frame and brought out the dummy he had constructed out of rags and wire clothes hangers earlier that evening. He placed the dummy on the bed and pulled the blanket up to the pillow, so it would appear to anyone walking by that he had fallen asleep with his head under the covers. Garrow had fixed it so the guard wouldn't be suspicious at the sight. Each night over the past few weeks he had made certain that the covers were over his head when the guard conducted bed check.

Garrow walked to the open doorway of his room. (Because the authorities figured that inmates at Fishkill were too old or too incapacitated to attempt an escape, they allowed the doors to be left unlocked at night.) He checked both ways to be certain that the hallway was deserted. Then he proceeded silently to the portico halfway down the corridor. Once there, he withdrew from inside the tan windbreaker he was carrying a foot-long piece of lumber he had stolen from the prison wood shop. He placed the length of wood between two of the decorative window bars and grasped it with both hands. With a couple of quick twists, he spread the bars far enough apart so he could crawl through. When he was out on the porch, he took the time to bend the metal bars back into place so that his escape wouldn't be too readily detected when the guard made bed check.

Limping severely, Garrow ran for the fourteen-foot-tall chain link fence located some fifty yards from the building. As he moved across the neatly trimmed lawn, he glanced up and smiled. He was lucky. The night had held clear and warm. By the time he reached the fence, he was sweating heavily with the pain and exhaustion of working his bad leg so hard. Without breaking stride, he threw himself against the fence. Using mostly his right arm, which had become awesomely strong as a result of over five years of favoring his withered, atrophied left arm, Garrow scaled the chain link barrier. Upon reaching the top, he placed his jacket over the coils of barbed wire and rolled over it. He grunted as he hit the ground. Flashes of pain shot up his left leg, which still carried fragments of the deer slugs that had brought him down in the 1973 manhunt.

He crouched just outside the fence and surveyed his surroundings. He had studied the terrain hundreds of times over the past couple of months while sitting in his wheelchair in the portico of his building. Some twenty feet beyond the fence and running for tens of miles in all directions were dense woods and underbrush so thick you would practically have to step on a man to spot him. It was Garrow's kind of terrain.

As fast as his bad leg would allow, Garrow ran low to the ground across the open field and slid into the underbrush. Once safely in the woods, he found a spot from which he could see the prison and waited.

The most feared killer in New York State history, whom most everyone, including the Department of Corrections officials who had arranged his transfer to Fishkill, believed to be a harmless cripple, was at large again.

28

September 9, 1978

Mary Armani watched with undisguised irritation as her husband lit a cigarette.

"You know that I love one with my morning coffee," Armani said, in answer to his wife's look. "Besides, I only smoke a couple a day. I'm doing the best I can."

"I guess a couple a day beats the three packs you used to inhale," his wife said with a tone of resigned pity. She had learned a long time ago that her husband was bullheaded. Once he talked himself into something, there was no stopping him.

Armani adjusted his tie and gulped the rest of his coffee. "Best be going."

"See you around five o'clock?" she asked.

"Around five," he answered.

Armani pushed to his feet. He was reaching toward the Formica counter for his briefcase when the doorbell sounded.

"I'll get it," Mary closed the collar of her terrycloth robe and walked through the kitchen to the back door.

Armani busied himself with slipping into his suit jacket. He was about to head into the garage to get his car when Mary reappeared. Walking behind her was Henry McCabe of the BCI.

"Henry, what the hell are you doing here?" a surprised Armani asked.

"Came by to talk with you," the detective answered. He hadn't seen Armani since before the lawyer had suffered his heart attack. McCabe noticed immediately the change in Armani's appearance. Armani no longer had that look of coiled power. He had aged considerably. His face was more angular. Some of the fire was gone from his gray eyes. His shoulders were less square, and he seemed to have lost at least twenty pounds since the Garrow trial.

"You got any more of that coffee?" McCabe asked, covering his chagrin over Armani's appearance. He reached out and pumped the lawyer's hand.

"Sure." Armani pulled a mug down from the cupboard and poured coffee for himself and McCabe.

"How are you feeling?" McCabe asked, taking a chair at the kitchen table. "I heard about your heart attack . . . I'm sorry."

"Hey, I'm doing all right. It's just taken me a long time to get my strength back."

"No more big murder trials?"

"Been layin' off those for a while."

"Heard you been appearing all over the country on the Garrow thing," McCabe said.

"No big deal. I've spoken at a couple of law school symposiums. Have actually turned down more invitations than I accepted. The doctor told me not to push it. But I've enjoyed the ones I've done."

"From what I've been told, the legal community has finally gotten around to calling you a hero for the fight you put up to protect Garrow's right of confidentiality."

"Don't know about the hero business," Armani answered, slightly embarrassed, "but at least they're not throwing rocks at me anymore."

"I always thought the media and the public gave you a raw deal," McCabe added.

"How about you, Henry? How'd you feel about Belge and me not telling you where those bodies were? Especially since you were going nuts trying to find those girls?"

"I have to admit that at the time I didn't particularly like what you did. But deep in my mind I always respected your right to hold back the information your client had revealed to you."

Armani nodded, then asked, "How are things with you and with the world of cops and robbers?"

"Never any shortage of crime; you know that, Frank. Next year, though, I'll be hanging up my jockstrap. I turn fifty-five, and they let me out to pasture."

"With your pension, you got it made."

"Hell," McCabe replied with mock irritation. "A cop's pension doesn't go very far. I'll have to get a job to supplement it. Or maybe I'll go to law school and get a license to steal."

Armani let out a loud laugh. He had always liked McCabe.

"Haven't heard much from Belge since the grand jury charges against him were dismissed," McCabe said.

"You knew he got suspended from practicing law?"

"Read it in the paper," McCabe replied. "My memory serves me right, he got it for mishandling one of his client's estates."

"That's it," Armani replied with disgust. "A bum rap, if you ask me."

"Where is he these days?" McCabe asked.

"Not sure. Last I heard he was in the Virgin Islands."

"Too bad he's not practicing law. He was one brilliant counselor."

"The best," Armani answered. He stared unseeing out over his back yard. "Belge was like a great fighter who took on all comers. All those big cases took it out of him. Afraid he answered the bell one too many times."

"Speaking of answering the bell one too many times, Holcombe sure got his comeuppance."

"You could say that," Armani answered. Holcombe had been forced to resign as Onondaga County district attorney the year before after being found guilty of drunk driving. A more serious charge of sexually abusing his secretary on the same night he was apprehended for drunk driving had been dropped. The dismissal of the sexual abuse charge had raised a furor within Syracuse's liberal establishment, especially since Holcombe was fined just $200 for the entire incident.

"Guess it could've been a lot worse on him," McCabe added, his coy expression indicating his understatement.

"Are you saying that the blindfold on the statue of Lady Justice doesn't block her entire vision, Henry?" Armani raised his eyebrows to emphasize the playful provocation in his question.

McCabe refused the bait.

Mary Armani left the kitchen sink, where she had been rinsing dishes, and walked over to the table. "Seems to me that just about everyone associated with the Garrow case has suffered some kind of tragedy," she interjected.

Armani and McCabe glanced at one another and waited for her to continue.

"The case sent Belge on the bender he's still on," she said. "William Intemann was defeated in his bid for reelection as Hamilton County district attorney. Holcombe had his trouble and was forced to resign. You practically went bankrupt, Frank, then had a heart attack. Plus there was the business of getting turned down for the U.S. attorney job."

"What was that about?" McCabe asked.

Armani threw his wife a hard look. "I put in for the vacant U.S. attorney slot. After I got turned down, a couple of guys on the selection committee told me privately that I'd been passed over because I had represented Garrow."

"Then there's Judge Marthen," Mary continued.

"Marthen? What happened to him?" McCabe was surprised.

"He's got cancer," Armani informed him solemnly. "Bad, I hear."

"Damn!" McCabe ran a hand through his slicked-down hair. "A real shame. He's a helluva guy."

"You ask me," Mary finished, "Garrow is just plain evil. He's tainted about everyone he's touched."

"Guess you can add his kid to that list," McCabe offered.

"What do you mean, Henry?" Armani asked.

"Take it you haven't seen the paper or the TV this morning," the detective said, his eyes narrowing.

"Stuff upsets me too much, so I pass on the news. What'd I miss?"

"Garrow escaped last night. His kid has admitted to us that he smuggled a gun inside to his father, for which the kid will surely do some time."

"What?" Armani's eyes widened. "Garrow's on the loose again?"

"He broke out a window, climbed the fence, and walked into

the woods. I'm on my way down there this morning to help with the manhunt. The brass figures I knew Garrow pretty well."

"Oh my God!" Armani leaned back in his chair.

"The entire state is in an uproar. Already been a barrage of criticism against the Department of Corrections because they transferred Garrow to Fishkill. Perry Duryea is trying to make the most of the escape in order to get elected governor in the fall. He's claiming that Garrow's transfer smells of a fix, the way Garrow dropped his lawsuit against the state right after he got sent to Fishkill. People are also screaming for reinstatement of the death penalty to keep anything like this from happening again."

Armani shook his head. "I can't believe the bastard actually got out of Fishkill."

"A kid could break out of there, Frank. Our problem now is to catch him. The woods near Fishkill aren't nearly as rugged and dense as the Adirondacks, but it's still gonna be tough to nail him."

"He drove you guys crazy the last time."

"You know anything that might help us bring him in?"

"Let me see," Armani mused. He took a moment to remember back to 1973 to see if he could recall some of the tactics Garrow had told him about using to elude the police. "My guess, Henry, is that he'll hang out right around the prison. He likes to stay put until he figures what you'll do. And I'd be willing to bet anything that he's got a radio. He'll be monitoring news reports about the manhunt, blockades, and all of it."

McCabe's eyes narrowed. Armani had given him something useful to work with.

"He once told me that he would hole up in the underbrush until the cops gave up the search in that area and pulled out," Armani continued. "That's how he broke out of your dragnet up in Speculator."

"Smart bastard," McCabe concluded. "What about his health? How strong is he?"

"Only thing I know is that while he was in Dannemora he was secretly exercising his arm and leg. I lost track of him after that."

"Appreciate the information, Frank."

Armani nodded.

"One more thing," McCabe added, quietly serious. "We found a hit list in his room—people he planned to waste if he ever got out."

"So?"

"Your name is on the list, Frank. Along with Belge, Judge Marthen, Norm Mordue, and Bill Intemann."

"You've got to be kidding!" Armani glanced at his wife, noted her stunned look, then reached for a cigarette.

"Now, don't get excited," McCabe admonished. "We both know that the chances of him ever making it to Syracuse are slim. But as a precaution, I'm assigning a detail of officers to keep an eye on you. Like I said, it's just a precaution. I personally don't think you have anything to worry about."

"When am I *ever* going to be rid of that guy?" Armani asked, more of himself than of McCabe.

"I think I understand how you feel," McCabe answered as he stood.

"Your name on that list?" Armani asked.

McCabe waved him off. "I should have a hundred bucks for every guy I sent away who promised to kill me. Now I'd best be going. Have to catch a plane for downstate."

Armani leaned forward to get to his feet. The BCI investigator held up his hand. "You both sit still. I can find my own way out."

"Goodbye, Henry," Armani said.

"You take care, willya, Frank? And don't worry about anything. They probably have already caught him." McCabe turned to Mary. "Nice to see you again, Mrs. Armani. Wish it could have been under more pleasant circumstances."

He walked out of the kitchen and pushed through the back door. Frank and Mary Armani sat in silence until they heard McCabe's car door slam.

"You don't look well, Frank," Mary said, noting her husband's pale complexion. "You okay?"

Armani took a few deep breaths. "Just some light pains in my chest."

Mary quickly left the table and grabbed the vial containing her husband's medication from over the sink.

"I hope you're not still planning on going into the office." She handed him two white capsules and a glass of water.

"I'll be okay in a couple of minutes."

He took his medication. Still sitting quietly at the table, Armani thought of something that had been left unsaid in his conversation with McCabe. During the 1973 manhunt, the cops had done their best to take Garrow alive so they might learn where he had stashed Susan Petz, on the slim chance that the girl might still be alive. Garrow didn't have that kind of life insurance going for him now; he might not be so lucky this time.

29

·•·

Later That Morning

M<small>CCABE ARRIVED</small> at Fishkill Correctional Facility a little before noon. The area just outside the prison's chain link fence looked like an army encampment. There were tents, four-wheel-drive trucks, and men in fatigues everywhere. McCabe set out immediately for the large, round tent in the middle of the compound that served as the search command post headquarters.

"Where's Lieutenant Walker?" McCabe asked a uniformed man standing near the tent entrance.

The trooper pointed across the crowded tent. The husky six-foot-six Lieutenant Walker, an ever-present cigar stuck in his mouth, was talking to a group of searchers. Walker, a state trooper, was coordinating the two-hundred-man search team of troopers and Correction Emergency Response Team (CERT) members.

McCabe detoured by a large stainless steel thermos to grab a cup of coffee, then made his way across the tent.

"How's it going, lieutenant?" McCabe asked.

"Hello, Henry." Walker answered out of the side of his mouth as if he had been interrupted. He didn't seem especially pleased that McCabe had arrived at Fishkill to monitor the manhunt.

"Got anything?" McCabe inquired, reading the lieutenant's mood.

"Nothing yet. We got men combing the woods in elbow-to-elbow formation. Roadblocks are up on all roads leading out of the area, and we're searching every house within a couple miles of the prison."

"Good," McCabe said. "Any guesses as to where he might be?"

Walker moved his jaw in such a way his cigar crawled to the other corner of his mouth. "Being as he had about an eight-hour head start, I figure he's left the area. We're getting reports of sightings from as far away as Syracuse."

No matter how slim the possibility, the idea that Garrow could have somehow made it to Syracuse scared the hell out of McCabe. That was where he would head if he were going to attempt to make good on the intention to eliminate the people on his hit list. Armani and Mordue lived in Syracuse. Judge Marthen, William Intemann, and Francis Belge lived within an hour of there, though McCabe now knew that Belge was probably in the Virgin Islands.

"Any substantiation to any of the sightings?" the BCI investigator asked.

"Negative," Walker responded. "Just part of the hysteria that Garrow has caused. People all over the state are panicking. I've got reports of people as far away as Vermont abandoning their summer homes and heading for the cities."

McCabe thought the scene a replay of 1973, when Garrow had paralyzed the entire Adirondack region. "My feeling is that he's still in this area, probably right around the prison somewhere."

"How do you figure?" Walker challenged.

"Just a hunch. He's been in that wheelchair too long, so, unless he's got a car, his stamina isn't good enough to take him very far on foot. Plus Garrow's medical reports state that the tendons in his left leg were severed when he took those slugs in seventy-three. The leg is shorter than his right one, and he only has limited use of it."

"I don't agree with you that he's still around here," Walker said. "I'm for moving our search away from the prison, fanning out to the adjoining countryside."

"Not yet," McCabe cautioned.

"He ain't here, I'm tellin' you. We've been over every square foot of ground around this prison."

"Then go over every square foot of it again," McCabe said impatiently. Then he backed off a bit. "Look, Mike, despite what the press would have us believe, the guy's not some sort of a phantom who can walk through steel walls and across water. I'm telling you that he's layin' low right around here, waiting for us to move out of the area so he can make his break for a car. And if he gets a car, we're really screwed. The thruway is only three miles from here. He gets across the Beacon-Newburgh bridge, we'll never catch him. You can bet he won't pull a bonehead move like run to his sister's house this time. I say he's here, and here is where I suggest you look."

Walker chewed angrily on his cigar and glared down at McCabe.

The BCI investigator held his ground. He wasn't about to relent, not after Armani had tipped him to how Garrow liked to stick in one place until his searchers gave up and left the area. He wasn't going to get by with that one again. McCabe wasn't about to be fooled the same way twice.

"Hope you're right, Henry," Lieutenant Walker grunted, and walked away.

For the following three days, while two hundred heavily armed searchers, many leading bloodhounds or German shepherds, tramped through the woods surrounding Fishkill Correctional Facility, Robert Garrow lay hidden in the underbrush not five hundred yards from the prison fence. When the searchers got close enough that he heard them fighting through the nearby growth, Garrow simply covered himself with leaves and brush and waited until they passed by a few feet from where he was hiding.

But Garrow made a major mistake. Late on the second night he was at large, he ventured away from his hiding place to check the location of the police command post. He lost his pocket radio somewhere in the underbrush. Not only did this rob him of his ears to the outside world, now he also ran the risk that one of the searchers would run across the radio and his position would be betrayed. But with the searchers concentrating their efforts on the sector in which he was hiding, Garrow had no choice but to stay put. He knew that making a break for it on his bum leg would result in his being spotted in the open and caught.

On the afternoon of the third day Garrow was free, after reports that he had been seen as far away as Canada, a CERT team member discovered Garrow's radio. Even at that, it took almost four hours for the prison authorities to ascertain that it belonged to the fugitive. Once that was verified, Lieutenant Walker concentrated his men in the area in which the radio had been found.

For the balance of that afternoon, CERT team members and state troopers, many with tracking dogs, marched side by side in a long line through the underbrush. Despite news of the discovery of Garrow's radio, most of the searchers had lapsed into a mood of inattentiveness. Many discounted the importance of the discovery, believing Garrow had dropped the radio the first night he had escaped and that he was long gone from the area. Some of the men had even taken to kidding one another about how many times they had searched a particular piece of ground. Occasionally someone would peek into a tangle of underbrush and call, "Are you in there, Mr. Garrow? If so, please come out. We want to go home for dinner."

At approximately six o'clock Monday, September 11th, a detail of weary searchers led by CERT officer Dominic Arena was making its final sweep through their designated area. The men moved slowly, as if just going through the motions so they could be done for the day. Arena noticed a quick movement in the brush immediately to his left. Not more than five feet from the search team, Robert Garrow leaped suddenly to his feet, then dropped to one knee, took aim with his pistol, and fired. Arena, the search detail's point man, fell, wounded. The other officers opened fire, and a deafening roar of gunfire shattered the early evening stillness. Garrow pitched over backwards, his torn body jumping and twisting as he hit the ground.

It was over in seconds; the woods once again fell still. The search team members, rifles at the ready as if expecting Garrow to jump up and continue the firefight, approached their quarry. One of the men bent cautiously and touched Garrow's throat, looked up, and offered a satisfied nod.

30

That Evening

FRANK ARMANI arrived home from his office just after five o'clock and took a short nap. After awakening, he spent a few minutes talking with his two daughters. Debbie was scheduled to leave for Oswego the next day, where she would begin her senior year of college. Dorina was to enter Boston College at the end of the week.

A little after six o'clock the Armani family sat down to a dinner of chicken sauteed in tomatoes and onions, one of Frank's favorite dishes. Dessert was a chocolate cake ablaze with fifty-one candles, carried to the table amid a hearty offering of "Happy Birthday" by Mary and the two girls. After opening his gifts—dress shirts from Debbie and Dorina and a cashmere sweater from Mary—and while his wife cleared the dishes, Frank Armani rose from the table and walked into the living room. He parted the front window drapes, glanced out, then rejoined the others at the kitchen table.

"What is it, Frank?" Mary asked, noting the troubled expression on her husband's face.

"The state car isn't there," he answered. "The cops who were watching the house are gone."

"What does that mean?" Debbie asked.

"I don't know," Armani answered. "Did Henry McCabe call while I was asleep?"

"Nobody called," Mary answered.

Frank twisted in his chair and turned on the portable color television situated on the Formica counter dividing the kitchen from the eating area. The local news was just finishing up. The newscaster revealed that a commission had been appointed by Governor Carey to investigate the reasons for Garrow's transfer to Fishkill and to ascertain how he had managed to escape so easily from the prison. Commissioner of Corrections Richard Hongisto, under extreme criticism for how he had handled Garrow's incarceration, had offered his resignation to the governor, who had reluctantly accepted it. Hongisto's resignation added to the list of prison officials who had lost their jobs since Garrow had escaped. In addition to the guard who had conducted the bed check in Garrow's building the night he had fled, two high-ranking administrators at Fishkill Correctional Facility had been fired in the past two days.

"That madman Garrow could topple the state government," Armani muttered while staring at the television. "He just might cause Carey to lose the November election."

Mary Armani appeared at the table. She slid a cup of coffee and a plateful of cake and ice cream in front of her husband.

"Am I allowed to eat this?" Armani asked, hungrily eyeing the dessert.

"On your birthday we make an exception to the doctor's rule against sweets," his wife said with a smile. "Besides, if those cigarettes haven't killed you, a piece of chocolate cake and a little ice cream sure can't hurt."

The national news came on as Armani, his wife, and daughters dug into their dessert. Roger Mudd was filling in for the vacationing Walter Cronkite. His first news story prompted Armani to drop his fork to the table.

"Word has just been received," Mudd began, "that Robert Garrow, the convicted mass murderer from upstate New York, has been fatally wounded by state police outside Fishkill Prison, the prison from which he had mysteriously vanished three days ago."

"My God," Armani said as an old photo of Garrow appeared on the screen.

"Quiet," Mary ordered.

"Garrow, as you might remember," Mudd continued, "was involved in one of the most bizarre criminal cases in United States history. It was Robert Garrow who in 1974 while on the

witness stand during his trial for murdering Philip Domblewski, a young camper from Schenectady, shocked the courtroom by admitting to having also committed three other
murders and seven rapes. At the close of the day's courtroom
proceedings, Garrow's attorneys, Frank Armani and Francis
Belge [Armani's and Belge's photos appeared on the screen],
both of Syracuse, dropped a bombshell by revealing that they
had known for almost a year that Garrow had committed the
murders. In fact, the lawyers had secretly viewed and photographed two victims' bodies, Susan Petz, twenty, of Skokie,
Illinois, and Alicia Hauck, sixteen, of Syracuse, in August 1973,
several months before the authorities were able to locate the
bodies. In the months between the time the lawyers viewed the
bodies and the authorities found them, the father of one of the
victims visited one of the lawyers to ask if Garrow might have
been involved with his daughter's disappearance. The lawyer,
Frank Armani, put the man off, even though the girl's parents
were treating the case as that of a runaway and advertising
pleas for their daughter to come home. At the time, of course,
Frank Armani knew that both girls were dead, but he still kept
silent, although not with an easy conscience. Frank Armani
said, 'Keeping the horrible secret was enough to drive you insane.' Armani and Belge were caught between two conflicting
duties. On one hand, as citizens and officers of the court, they
had a strong legal obligation to report a serious crime—two serious crimes, in fact. But on the other hand, as advocates for
their client, they had an equally strong professional obligation
to safeguard information he had given them in professional
confidence. They opted to fulfill the latter responsibility at the
expense of the former.

"This of course wasn't the first time these ethical responsibil-
ities of a lawyer have come into conflict. But rarely has the
problem been posed so starkly as it was in the Garrow case.
This case may be a landmark, in the opinion of qualified pro-
fessionals. And even today, with Robert Garrow killed outside
Fishkill Correctional Facility and with his two attorneys
absolved of any criminal or professional wrongdoing by an
Onondaga County grand jury and by the American Bar Association, the question is still wide open. The public and the legal
profession are still strongly divided on the issue of how far an
attorney may go in protecting his client's right of confidenti-

ality. On the one hand, an attorney is an officer of the law, sworn to uphold it fully. On the other, he's the committed advocate for a client whose interests often may clash with the law. Which obligation comes first? It is an emotionally charged issue that may not be resolved for some time to come."

As Roger Mudd moved on to another story, Armani leaned back in his chair and closed his eyes. His wife and daughters watched with concern as Armani's lips moved in silence.

Mary moved to her husband's side and put her arms around his shoulders. "Are you okay, Frank?"

"Yeah, I'm all right," Armani answered. He opened his tear-filled eyes and looked up at his wife. "This may sound cruel, but I was just thanking God for putting that poor sick devil out of his misery."

Debbie and Dorina glanced across the table at one another, then moved to join their mother in embracing their father.

"Does this mean it's finally over for you?" Mary asked, the emotion rising in her throat.

"I hope so, Mary. I really hope so."

Mary and the girls returned to their chairs and resumed eating their dessert.

"I just thought of something," Frank said, pushing to his feet. "I'll be right back."

"Is there anything I can do?" Mary leaned forward in preparation to stand.

Armani waved her off. "It's okay. I'll only be a minute."

Armani walked downstairs to the basement of his house and into his private study. He headed straight for the bookshelf, out of which he pulled a leather storage case. He opened it and located the cassette tape he wanted. He stepped across the room to his stereo player and inserted the tape. After turning on the power, and pressing the *play* button, he sat in the leather armchair next to the stereo.

The sound of Armani's voice and that of Robert Garrow, Jr., son of the slain killer, broke the silence. Armani leaned over and pressed the *fast forward* button. He held it depressed for a few seconds, then released it. When he was satisfied that the tape was at the right spot of the interview, he reclined back in his armchair.

"Do you think your father killed Philip Domblewski?" Armani's voice sounded out of the speakers.

"No," Robert Garrow, Jr., answered.

"Why do you say that?" Armani asked.

"Because it didn't make any sense for him to leave the other three campers alive for witnesses. If it was me, I would have killed all four of them," young Garrow answered.

There was a moment of silence on the tape. Armani remembered the pause well. He had been so shocked by the kid's answer that he had been at a loss for words. Then the tape picked up with Armani's voice.

"Do you carry a weapon on you, Robert?"

"A Buck knife," the boy answered. "Plus I have a gun at home."

"Would you ever use the knife or the gun on anyone?"

"Only if someone threatened me . . . or if they got me mad enough."

Frank Armani reached up from the armchair and flipped off the cassette player. He sat in silence for a few long moments, thinking about what he had just heard.

Then he reached into his pocket and withdrew the letter he had received that day. It was one of a constant stream of hate letters he had received since the Garrow trial. Armani had gotten them from all over the United States and Canada. This one was postmarked in Paramus, New Jersey. Like all of the others, it was unsigned and bore no return address. On the single sheet of white paper was written:

> May you know the pain and anguish
> that you gave to
> Mr. & Mrs. Petz
> Mr. & Mrs. Hauck

Armani refolded the letter and stuck it back into the envelope. He pivoted in his chair and pulled open the middle drawer of his desk. He reached in and touched the loaded pistol, just to make sure it was still there. This was one of three handguns he had purchased during the early days of the Garrow trial, after he had learned that there was a contract out on his life. He kept another in the glove compartment of his car, the third in his desk at his office.

Frank Armani closed the desk drawer, leaned back in his chair, and shut his eyes.

Epilogue

T HE READER might care to know what has happened to the principal characters in this real-life drama since September 11, 1978, the day Robert Garrow was gunned down outside Fishkill Correctional Facility.

Frank Armani had another heart attack in 1981; presently, his health has improved, though he is somewhat restricted in his activities. Despite many of his former clients' never returning, Armani has rebuilt his Syracuse law practice. His family is intact. Mary sells residential real estate in the western suburb of Syracuse in which the Armanis reside; Debbie lives in southern California, where she is an actress; Dorina is in her second year of law school.

Francis Belge, suspended from practicing law, lives in Florida.

Robert Garrow is buried in Oakwood Cemetery. His gravesite is only a few hundred feet from where he hid Alicia Hauck's body.

Edith Garrow works for an insurance company in Syracuse.

Michelle Garrow, Robert's daughter, married the boy next door. She and her husband live in downstate New York under a cloak of anonymity.

Robert Garrow, Jr., was sentenced to four years in prison for smuggling the gun in to his father at Fishkill Correctional Facility. During the trial, the presiding judge strongly suggested that Robert, Jr., change his name and, once he had served his time, start life over. Young Garrow failed to heed the judge's advice. Presently he lives in Syracuse, where he has been in and out of trouble with the law.

Henry McCabe retired from the New York State Police Department. He and his wife reside in the Albany area, near Saratoga Racetrack, where McCabe works as a security guard during the summers.

Judge George Marthen died of cancer recently in Lake Pleasant.

Jon Holcombe has left political life. He practices law in Syracuse.

William Intemann practices law in Speculator. He also owns a restaurant with his wife.

Norman Mordue is an Onondaga County Court judge.

For the people of the Lake Pleasant area, life goes on with the unhurried, serene pace indigenous to that mountain resort area. And yet some ten years after the murders, manhunt, and trial, each person we interviewed recalled with uncommon accuracy and emotions the events and the mood of the region during the Robert Garrow affair. It was as though the fear, relief, and excitement of the mid-1970s all occurred just yesterday. The horror and the circuslike atmosphere of a decade ago have been indelibly etched into the hearts and minds of the residents of the Adirondack Mountains.

Source Notes

THE RESEARCH NECESSARY to write *Privileged Information* was massive and exhaustive, as is usual whenever a writer attempts to recreate a complex, interrelated series of events that occurred some years earlier. Memory tends to blend fact and fiction; an individual's perception of past events can sometimes become distorted by how that person saw things at the time, or how he or she would have preferred that situation to have been resolved. Especially if that individual is recounting some painful memory. For that reason we found it necessary to check and cross-check certain details relating to Robert Garrow's life, his manhunt, trial and their aftermath.

Garrow's chief defense counsel, Frank H. Armani, came to know the killer intimately, and was touched by nearly every aspect of the controversy. The fact that he co-authored *Privileged Information* made researching this book less laborious than it would have been otherwise.

Fortunately for us, the Garrow case was practically constant front-page news in most New York State newspapers; one batch of newspaper and magazine clippings on the manhunt, trial and aftermath weighed over 40 pounds. From these accounts, despite the occasional discrepancy between what was reported and what actually happened, we were able to corroborate much of what we learned from interviewing the main characters in this true life drama. In addition, the trial tran-

213

script's 2,000-plus pages afforded us huge amounts of details and critical information.

The principals of the Garrow case we interviewed are far too many to list here. Some of them are: Robert and Margaret Garrow, the murderer's parents, who offered their viewpoints on why their son became the deranged person he did (for which, incidentally, they claimed no responsibility); Judge George Marthen, who, although seriously ailing from the cancer which eventually killed him, was extremely generous with his time and wisdom; Henry McCabe, who was refreshingly candid about his perspective of the manhunt, trial and Garrow's eventual escape from Fishkill Correctional Facility; Frank Armani's wife, Mary, who proved to be an invaluable resource in recounting the pressures the lawyer and his family underwent, and still undergo, as a result of the ordeal; Hamilton County Sheriff Parker, who willingly shared his experiences as Garrow's jailer in the months before, and during, the murder trial; John Zeiser, owner of Zeiser's Inn in Speculator, NY—trial headquarters for the defense and the press—who offered his views on the mood of the locals during that highly charged, emotional period.

We reviewed the defense counsels' notes of their interviews with Robert Garrow; we listened to 50 hours of cassette tapes of Armani's and Belge's interviews with Garrow, the murderer's wife and children, and his sisters; we read the voluminous reports of the various psychiatrists who evaluated Robert Garrow's mental condition for the purpose of testifying at his trial; we reviewed the transcript of the Onondaga County grand jury hearing that investigated Frank Armani's conduct in the Alicia Hauck case; we studied the articles that appeared in professional legal journals, along with transcripts of the symposiums conducted by various law schools and bar associations debating Armani's professional ethics in maintaining Robert Garrow's right to confidentiality.

We also visited many of the key sites relative to the case. On a hot, humid August afternoon, we retraced the path Armani and Belge had taken when they'd searched for the body of Susan Petz. En route, we experienced the macabre phenomenon that was the channel of frigid air that belched from the abandoned Republic Steel Iron mine and flowed in a five-foot-wide channel down the mountainside. We stepped off the area in Oakwood Cemetery, where Robert Garrow hid the body of Alicia Hauck. And late one night we drove to Speculator for the purpose of walking the campsite from which Garrow abducted the four campers. When we were unable to secure a motel room, we camped near the spot where Philip Domblewski was stabbed to death. It was there we heard the same sounds, and smelled the same smells, the four young campers did only hours before Robert Garrow crept unseen and unheard into their campground.